F.J. Bohan

BARBED WIRE, BARRICADES, AND BUNKERS

The Free Citizen's Guide to Fortifying the Home Retreat

Paladin Press · Boulder, Colorado

Other books by F.J. Bohan:
Living on the Edge: A Family's Journey to Self-Sufficiency

A very special thanks to the great people at the U.S. Army Heritage and Education Center and the Army Heritage Trail in Carlisle, Pennsylvania, who let us photograph many of their outdoor displays. The U.S. Army's preeminent museum and research complex, the center is both free and open to the public.

Barbed Wire, Barricades, and Bunkers:
The Free Citizen's Guide to Fortifying the Home Retreat
by F.J. Bohan

Copyright © 2012 by F.J. Bohan

ISBN 13: 978-1-61004-830-9
Printed in the United States of America

Published by Paladin Press, a division of
Paladin Enterprises, Inc.
Gunbarrel Tech Center
7077 Winchester Circle
Boulder, Colorado 80301 USA
+1.303.443.7250

Direct inquiries and/or orders to the above address.

PALADIN, PALADIN PRESS, and the "horse head" design
are trademarks belonging to Paladin Enterprises and
registered in United States Patent and Trademark Office.

Visit our website at www.paladin-press.com.

Contents

•

Warning

•

Some of the projects found in this book require experience with construction. Whenever planning an excavation or shelter that depends on significant weight-bearing structures (such as those with sandbags or other cover built into the roof design), exercise caution to prevent injury to yourself and any inhabitants.

Introduction

•

With an anticipated economic collapse and the standard march-to-war response of government, the only growth most Americans see today is in the uncertainty of the future. This uncertainty has gained strength, and the uptick in gun sales alone seems to indicate that it has become a major concern in this country. Americans may not know exactly what the future holds, but we do know it isn't pretty and those who are able are preparing for the worst. At all levels of our society you'll find preppers or, simply put, those preparing for tougher times.

Although the idea of having a survival retreat has recently gone mainstream again, it is nothing new to Americans; anyone who lived through the Cuban Missile Crisis or has seen any number of apocalyptic movies is aware of the average American's ideal home bunker. We want a spacious underground condo with all the modern luxuries and a hardened door with a big lock that can be closed from the inside. Anything less, for many Americans, just won't do. Even preppers can be a bit out of touch with reality.

So, here we are: a nation bankrupted by overspending with a government completely out of touch with the people, realizing the coming need for bunkers but putting comfort and convenience so far ahead of practicality that the end result is beyond our financial means to achieve.

We can't just crawl into our bunkers, lock the doors, and watch old movies until the world's problems disappear. It was crawling into our retreats that most likely got us into this situation in the first place. Reality will have us taking a far more active and physical role in the future if we are to survive.

The biggest difference in what we face this time is in the potential threat. During the Cold War, we were certain the threat was a godless and immoral foreigner, either a socialist, fascist, or communist, threatening us and our children from overseas. Today we realize that the threat is already here, working for our government and teaching our children.

Each prepper has his own ideas about how bad things will get and who the threat is or will be. The most extreme levels of preparedness might include remote private retreats, hardened survival bunkers, and enough supplies to see the survivalist through several years of civil war, famine, and a complete socio-economic collapse, perhaps followed by a ground invasion of one or more former U.S. enemies looking to expand their own empires. Less extreme retreats are being fashioned in basements in towns and cities at the homes of preppers who don't want or simply cannot afford a country retreat. Preppers are doing what they can with what they have.

With the dollar's steady loss of buying power, the choices preppers make become more difficult, especially when it comes to the cost of building or fortifying their retreat in the expectation of threats. The hard costs of these types of improvements can quickly become too expensive. But good fortune has it that the art of fortification has seen multiple studies (many of which have already been paid for with your tax dollars) that can be used to formulate an effective plan for a home retreat.

The prepper considering a fortified position at a retreat differs from the squad, platoon, or battalion digging in to a combat zone. The prepper just doesn't have the resources the military has. Preppers must choose the correct location for each fortification improvement to the retreat and build it to last. No reinforcements will be coming, nor will an EVAC helicopter or rescue mission be deployed to get them out of a fight they can't handle.

When the SHTF, building materials and rental equipment will not be available. Now is the time to plan and build your retreat. A single hidden, secure structure may be enough protection for some preppers. But under the worst-case scenarios it may take several structures along with a few redundancies, a strong will to fight, and a good defensive plan to increase the odds of your survival against a superior force of intruders.

Each retreat will be different in its structures and natural features, but all have the potential of being defended and can indeed be successfully defended against ground attacks.

As you read this book and gain the understanding of how each structure can be used, you will start to apply these lessons to your own resources and situation. Some ideas may be beyond your ability to utilize, but you will hopefully find many within the scope of your talents and budget.

It is my hope that, no matter what your budget or resources, this book will serve to both inform and suggest ways to improve your retreat's or home's security and add to your own survivability in the adverse times ahead.

Chapter One

Barbed-Wire Fences

•

A good fence is a barrier that keeps people, animals, or vehicles out of areas you'd rather not have them in. Fences of some type or another have been used to define areas of real estate for centuries. Some of the earliest versions of fences include wooden stockade fences, stone walls, and even thick hedgerows. All of these types of barriers still serve as good fences today.

When the settlers came to the New World, they brought with them the same notions of fences that served them well in the old country. Stockade fences were built around the early settlements and also around animal pens and farm plots to control who or what was allowed in an area. They were commonly made from whichever local trees provided the longest lasting service. In many parts of the New World, stockades built from locust tree logs proved to last longer than other woods.

As time allowed, native plants were also used to create hedgerows to define areas and serve as fences. For those who could afford the time and labor, stone walls were also built.

Fencing is one of Western civilization's biggest pastimes. Having all but finished the fencing of Europe and getting a good start on fencing the settled portions of the eastern United States of America, we looked to the unfenced West.

As Americans set out to fence the West, they discovered that

Photo: The Army Heritage Trail at the U.S. Army Heritage and Education Center.

Stockade fences are sturdy, but depend
on having access to lots of timber.

there were few timbers from which to readily build stockade
fences and no shrubs or bushes suitable for cultivating adequate
hedgerows. Further, there were not nearly enough stones to
build the miles of fence that would be needed to properly en-
close such a large area. It was soon clear that the West was a lot
of wide-open space that, perhaps, could never be fenced. This
forced Americans to rethink our instinctive need to fence things
in. After contemplation, we devised a scheme whereby instead of
fencing *in* the West, we could use fewer resources by fencing
things *out* — sort of a divide-and-conquer approach. And so was
born the concept of open range, where property owners had to
fence out the cattle from their land.

Open range was the only way of the West for a few years until several relatively smart guys developed a thorny, or barbed, wire that could be used as fencing. There is some debate as to who actually invented barbed wire; however, the first patent was issued in 1867 to a man named Lucien B. Smith. Other variations followed soon after and almost immediately it was realized that the West could indeed be fenced in, and the task was begun.

Barbed wire is credited by many as being how the West was won. Having lived out West for many years, I can tell you that barbed wire didn't tame the West; it only tamed the men out West. After enough barbed wire had been run, the once carefree and roaming cowboy was soon fenced in and forced into a life of ranching.

This might have worked out fine for the cowboy except that the cattle didn't pay much attention to the barbed-wire fences. In fact, there is little that will stop a cow from its determined course. Barbed wire was simply a nuisance to the cattle and, at the end of the day, the cowboys-turned-ranchers had the added job of repairing barbed-wire fences. This was no easy task. Anyone who has had the opportunity to work with barbed wire will show you his or her scars as testament to how difficult it is to work with. Barbed wire has a way of twisting and snapping in just the wrong direction for your needs and catching your shirt, pants, or cheek with enough force to slice them up into a bloody mess.

The wire tends to retain the spring-tensile and shape of the original coiled roll and, even after years of being stretched and hung on a fence, when broken it snaps back on itself into a coiled tangle of wire. It didn't take long for ranchers out on the lower 40 to get caught in the garbled mess of barbed wire left by a determined steer who walked right through it.

Ranchers quickly learned that a barbed-wire fence does little to stop a cow, but it can create a tangled mess that can cut and trap a man to such an extent that he would require assistance to escape his situation. They had inadvertently discovered what would soon become the latest in modern warfare: the barbed-wire entanglement.

The discovery of the barbed-wire entanglement coincidently happened to come just in time to play a big role in World War I.

Two men inspect a deadly barricade made from sharpened
wooden posts and barbed wire in this WWI-era photograph.

A popular German left-wing writer of that time, Ernst Toller, laid
out the argument for barbed wire very neatly in one of his writ-
ings, although he most likely thought he was laying out the argument against it. As Toller explains: one night, soldiers heard the
cries of a dying man caught in the wire. As it turned out, the
man was one of theirs; perhaps he was a returning scout who
had been shot on his way back to report his findings, or maybe
he simply ventured out in the night to relieve himself. In any
event, his fellow soldiers, well protected in their trenches and
dugouts, could hear the agonized screams of their dying comrade
trapped in the wire just yards away. Most of them prayed that he

would just hurry up and die and stop his tormented cries. Two soldiers, wanting to help the situation, attempted a rescue but were quickly cut down by the Allies, who were clearly using the trapped man as both bait and as a demoralizing psychological operation against his fellow troops. The cries continued through the night and for three days until they were finally stopped by the poor man's death.

There are several lessons we should take from this tale. The first one is: Don't get caught in your own barbed-wire entanglement. Be certain to incorporate several escape routes that are well concealed from the attacker's positions. If or when you decide to leave your home, be sure your deterrents don't keep you trapped. Have a plan and an alternate route that will see you safely out of the wire. This can be done with tunnels, buried pipes, or even a hidden crawl trench that runs under the wire. Be sure to cache supplies outside the wire to retrieve later in such an event. At the very least, carry a good pair of wire cutters and leather gloves with you when you venture out through the wire.

The second lesson taken from the tale is to keep the wire in full view from your protected position. Not only do you want to be able to observe someone attempting to cut their way into your position, but you'll also want to know if someone is caught in the wire and be able to end any attempts at a rescue.

A third lesson is that a barbed-wire entanglement indeed works as a protective deterrent. A garbled mess of barbed wire will, at the very least, slow any threat down to a manageable pace or perhaps even stop the enemy long enough to drop him dead in his tracks.

Additionally, it is of note that psychological operations (PSYOP) have been used for many years in times of war. If you find that you have an opportunity to demoralize the threat by using one of their own, it should be seized. Make no mistake; your enemy will not only seize every opportunity you give him to run a PSYOP against you, your family, and friends, but actively create the opportunities to do so. War is hell.

Barbed wire is an essential tool for the defense of a home or retreat against an attack in troubled times. It, along with chain-

Heavy tanks and earth-moving equipment are the
barbed-wire entanglement's only true threat.

link or wire-mesh fence and multiple combinations of different
types of razor wire (such as concertina wire), makes up what is
commonly referred to as anti-personnel barriers. A well-pro-
tected home retreat will include anti-personnel barriers in addition to vehicle barriers and other structures.

Chapter Two

Barbed-Wire Entanglements

•

There are several recognized, uniform methods to construct an entanglement. They all share one common trait: they use a lot of wire. One of the best entanglements I have ever seen was simply a pile of discarded, rusty barbed wire. In fact, the more random the entanglements, the more effective they might be. Our military has a standard for converting four-strand barbed-wire cattle fences into entanglements. On paper it looks effective; however, it has a standard method to its construction and therefore a plan can be made ahead of time to defeat it.

The entanglement should be your own original work of art. It should use stout posts and stakes set firmly into the ground and have barbed wire strung to and fro at multiple levels and in all directions. Don't be afraid to use several types of wire. Several rows of concertina with a barbed wire woven in, out, and above and anchored to your posts at random points will make an entanglement that most intruders would rather bypass than traverse. Have some fun with it. When you're done, stand back and ask yourself, "Would I be able to get across that entanglement?" If your answer is yes, you need to add more wire.

Under some circumstances you may need to have a port or exit through your entanglement. One method is to construct a knife rest (or several of them). A knife rest is a portable wire

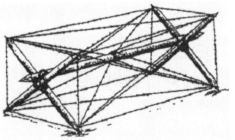

A knife rest is a mobile entanglement barrier that can be moved aside from the defender's side of the fence.

Foliage and barbed wire work together in this WWI barbed-wire entanglement.

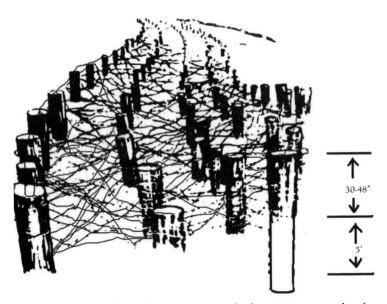

30-48"

5'

This log-post entanglement barrier serves as both an anti-personnel and an anti-vehicular barrier by combining the use of barbed wire and bollards. In this example, 8- to 10-inch diameter logs are buried 5 feet in the ground, sticking up 30 to 48 inches out of the ground. The posts are placed far enough apart to be too far for a man to jump from top to top. They can be made with logs or metal posts depending on what is available.

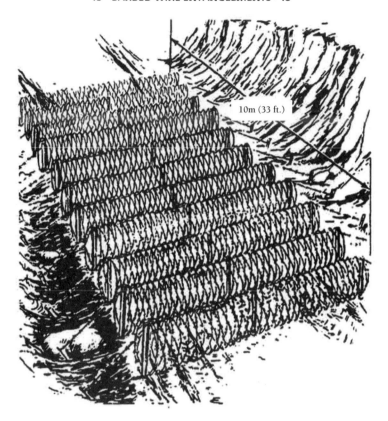

10m (33 ft.)

Concertina wire can provide a devastating obstacle to intruders.

entanglement that can be readily moved when anchored from the inside of a barrier. It is also used as a road block at manned posts to stop or control both foot and vehicle traffic. It can be made out of readily available materials and is simple to deploy.

Razor wire is barbed wire's younger and nastier brother. It will shred people and animals when properly placed and anchored. It, too, can be used to create effective barriers at the retreat. Concertina wire is available in many different coil diameters, from 18 to 60 inches, which allows smaller coils to be placed inside larger ones for a more effective barrier. Many types of flat-wire concertina wires are also nearly impossible to cut with conventional tools once deployed.

Chapter Three

Barbed-Wire Alternatives

•

Depending on your budget or situation, there are several alternatives to barbed wire you may consider. Given enough time for cultivation and growth, an effective perimeter deterrent can be made using native plants and bushes.

Brambles, such as rose bushes and blackberry or raspberry thickets, can serve just as well as a barbed-wire entanglement, either deterring or trapping a man attempting to pass through it. Many successful hedgerows have also been made from holly bushes and shrubs of the genus pyracantha, sometimes called firethorn. Given enough time, finding and cultivating the native thorny brush into a thicket or barrier can be an excellent low-cost alternative to barbed-wire barriers. It should be noted that hedgerows such as these cannot be seen through as easily as a barbed-wire entanglement and, therefore, should be placed at a location where your line of sight is not critical. It should also be combined with other measures, such as a dog pen set just inside the fence. There are several ornamental bushes that are extremely thorny and can be placed in staggered rows to create a natural fence and entanglement. The thorny-bush hedgerow has been protecting the common man from multiple threats for centuries.

When laying out the plan for your home retreat's protection, using a plant or bush entanglement whenever possible can also

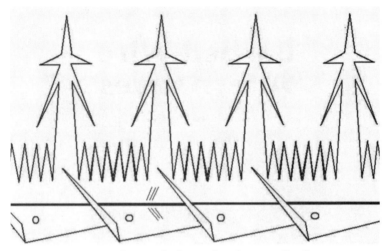

Razor spikes can be fastened to the tops of walls
and fences to deter would-be climbers.

help to keep your fortification low-profile and unnoticed by others around you.

A barbed-wire trip line, sometimes called "tangle foot," is also a useful tool in your home retreat's protection. Large, grassy areas either inside or outside your perimeter can be used to conceal barbed trip lines and wires set below the height of the grass but high enough to catch the shin of an approaching attacker. The wires should be placed at various angles of approach and randomly spaced. Tangle-foot trip wires are often used on the approach to a wire entanglement. Cow bells or metal coffee cans filled with pebbles and attached to the trip wires can offer an audible alert of an approaching attacker as well.

It is important to keep a map of your field, detailing its features, for future reference. You won't be cutting the grass anytime soon with the wires in place and may need to know the location of the wires and bells to determine if they have been altered or compromised.

Another excellent barbed-wire alternative is the razor spike, also known as the wall spike. It is a nasty metal strip formed into gothic and medieval shapes with razor-sharp points and edges and sold in convenient 60-inch strips. The razor-sharp points stick up from 2 to 4 inches and either cut or catch everything they touch. The strips can be placed at the tops of walls, fences, and buildings to deter unwanted guests from climbing over the top.

CHAIN-LINK AND WIRE-MESH FENCES

Chain-link fences or other wire-mesh fences used with barbed wire or razor wire, along with outriggers, can also form a fair anti-personnel barrier. These are commonly seen surrounding prisons, corrections institutions, and commercial property yards nationwide. You should note that they are rarely seen without a big dog or an armed guard nearby.

Chain-link fence is a low-cost, low-profile option for security of the home retreat. It can be readily modified at a later time when societal conditions take a turn for the worse. A 6-foot-tall chain-link fence can easily have outriggers and concertina wire added to its top, as well as a 3/4-inch wire cable woven through it to stop vehicular threats. There are also mesh fabrics available that can be added to a fence in order to provide a moderate level

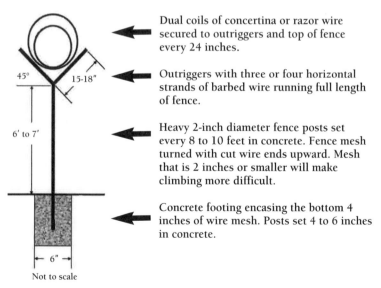

Dual coils of concertina or razor wire secured to outriggers and top of fence every 24 inches.

Outriggers with three or four horizontal strands of barbed wire running full length of fence.

Heavy 2-inch diameter fence posts set every 8 to 10 feet in concrete. Fence mesh turned with cut wire ends upward. Mesh that is 2 inches or smaller will make climbing more difficult.

Concrete footing encasing the bottom 4 inches of wire mesh. Posts set 4 to 6 inches in concrete.

Here is the suggested method of installing a wire-mesh or chain-link fence.

of visual concealment from outside the fence. These should only be used where they would not interfere with your line-of-sight observation of the area outside the fence.

Some general practices that should be considered when placing a fence include keeping the fence on clear, high ground so that the use of an adjacent hill or tree will not aid an intruder in climbing over the fence. Consider that utility poles and buildings can also be used as aids to jump fences. Keep the fence within view of your security posts.

Fences 6 feet or taller and topped with razor or barbed wire offer the highest level of anti-personnel security as fences go. Many fences are placed without the use of horizontal wires strung at the top and bottom of the mesh, but this makes it easier for intruders to push the mesh through and crawl under or over the fence. The best alternative to using a lower horizontal wire would be to pour a concrete footing the entire perimeter and actually set the bottom four inches of the fence in the concrete. This would greatly deter an intruder's ability to burrow under the fence and help keep the fence secure from natural erosion.

WIRE-MESH FENCE PRECAUTIONS

No one should rest his anti-personnel security concerns on a fence alone. While most fences do create a physical deterrent, and sometimes a psychological deterrent as well, there are many untrained attackers who will readily climb over or cut through your wire fence in a matter of minutes. Trained units would most likely be inside your perimeter in less than 30 seconds. There is not a wire fence anywhere that cannot be cut. Wire cutters can make cutting through the fence a breeze, and using a grappling hook and chain to pull down the barbed wire and outriggers will make it easier for intruders to climb over the fence. At best, the fence would offer you a few additional minutes to rally an effective response to the attack.

The only sure method of guaranteeing the success of the wire mesh fence is to have it under constant watch. This would require that the fence be placed in direct view of a secure post that is manned 24/7 or under the watch of closed-circuit television (CCTV) cameras. These options may not be reasonable for most preppers.

To gain additional minutes, wire fences must be used along with barbed-wire entanglements directly inside, outside, or on both sides of the fence, creating an effective anti-personnel barrier. Combining the use of the fence with a natural land feature can also greatly improve its effectiveness; placing a fence at the top of a knoll or along the ridge of a hill will add to its overall effectiveness.

Wire fences and anti-personnel barriers are only a part of a successful plan to deter a threat. Remember that a vehicle can easily defeat your fences and entanglements. Anti-vehicular barriers must also be used in your plan.

THE CABLE-REINFORCED CHAIN-LINK FENCE

A relatively low-cost method to increase the security of your chain-link fence is to weave two strands of 3/4-inch aircraft cable

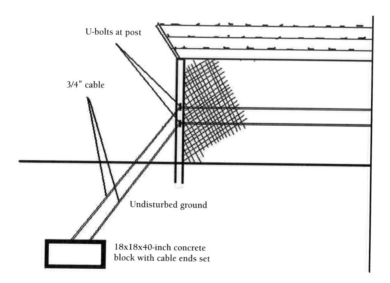

U-bolts at post

3/4" cable

Undisturbed ground

18x18x40-inch concrete block with cable ends set

Multiple crash tests have shown that a chain-link fence reinforced with dead-man anchor points made from 3/4-inch cable and placed as shown can successfully stop a 4,000-pound vehicle traveling at 50 mph. This type of fence should be enough of a deterrent for most home retreats.

or wire rope into the mesh at 2 feet, 6 inches and 2 feet, 11 inches above the ground level. The placement of the two strands of cable should run parallel and be pulled taut, but not under tension, with both ends being fastened to a buried dead-man anchor point. The anchor point should be buried at least 3 feet below the surface.

By adding this reinforcement to your chain-link fence you are effectively turning it into an anti-vehicular barrier that will deflect or stop light vehicles such as cars and light trucks. If you believe a larger vehicle presents a threat to your location, you can double the number of cables and the size of the dead-man for additional stopping power. Keep the vertical centerline of the cables at the 2-feet, 8-inch level. Increasing the number of fence posts will also increase the strength of the fence against vehicle threats. Place posts at every 4 feet rather than 8 or 10 feet.

TRIPLE-STRAND CONCERTINA FENCE

Another effective anti-personnel barrier is the triple-strand concertina fence. It is a simple barrier made from three rolls of ribbon razor wire anchored to the ground with stakes. You can use whatever material you have available for stakes as long as it can be driven into the ground and made secure. The more stakes you use the more secure and, therefore, more effective the barrier can be.

The two rows of stakes are staggered and set at the center of each of the lower rolls of concertina wire. A horizontal wire is run across the tops of each stake and anchored to it. Additionally, each of the concertina wire rolls should be tied to each other randomly with tie wire.

This fence is also an excellent complement to the inside of a chain-link fence and would greatly slow an intrusion.

Step 1. Work from the protected side of the barrier. Place front-row stakes and concertina and set horizontal wire. Use tie wire to anchor the concertina to the stakes as you go.

Enemy

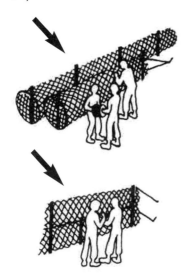

Step 2. Place the second row of stakes and concertina wire. Set horizontal anchor wire.

Step 3. Install the top row of concertina wire and rack it toward the inside lower-row stakes.

Installing concertina wire along a perimeter.

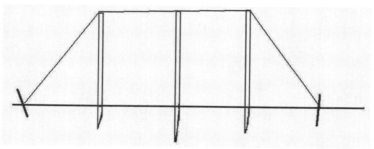

Detail of the horizontal anchor wire.

Chapter Four

Bollards

•

The term "bollard" originally referred to a post of metal or wood that was mounted on a wharf for the securing of mooring lines. The modern definition comes from the British who, when they needed a name for the low, sturdy posts they designed for traffic control obstacles, harkened back to their nautical past and referred to them as bollards. After all, you could moor a ship to them if there were water nearby, maybe.

The term "bollard" was quickly adopted for use by Americans. However, it is the Germans who really deserve credit for coming up with the modern concept. It should also be mentioned that the Germans had a much cooler name and design for the obstacles they called "dragon's teeth."

The dragon's teeth deployed by the Germans were sometimes less effective than they had hoped in stopping tanks and other vehicles. This was mainly due to the dragon's teeth not always being anchored to the ground and often being left unattended. They were indeed heavy and had both the shape and mass to deter traffic, but being left unattended allowed the teeth to be pulled from the path of the oncoming force.

Be certain to anchor your bollards to the ground in some manner or have them be of a size that is too big for your expected threat to readily move.

The Germans used bollards that tapered at
the top and dubbed them "dragon's teeth."

Whatever we call them, they are stout posts used as barriers
and obstacles. The bollard industry has exploded with the advent
of the so-called war on terrorism, and numerous variations have
been created that all meet a simple purpose: to stop or control
the movement of people or vehicles.

They are so commonplace today that you may not even
notice them as you go about your daily travels in town. They can
take any number of shapes, but all serve to direct you to where
they want you to be. They may want you to use a controlled
entrance or to keep off the grass, use a certain lane in traffic, or
have you walk past their facial recognition CCTV cameras on
your way to shop. Today's bollards can look like an ominous
security control device or be as innocent as a row of benches or a
group of concrete planters.

Isn't it nice that they want us to feel good about being cor-
ralled like cattle? Oh, what a nice bench they brought us and
such pretty plants and planters, too! It makes us want to smile
for the cameras. There are practical uses for bollards in and

A retail store makes use of plain, cylindrical
bollards near its front entrance.

around your home or retreat. You, too, can use them to control
traffic and direct what paths you want visitors to use. You can
make them out of wood, concrete, or even rocks, and they can
be combined with fences and other obstacles to stop the traffic of
your choice.

One word of caution: remember that care should be taken in
the proper placement of large bollards since any large concrete
object can be used as effective cover for an assault on your home.
Don't help them out!

The simplest bollards are stout posts used to keep vehicles
out of controlled areas. They have been used for many years by
embassies worldwide as a standard security measure to keep cars
and trucks from ramming buildings, guard posts, and entryways.

Any concrete object placed in a manner so as to stop vehicle
traffic can serve as a bollard. You can even form and pour your
own dragon's teeth. Many Americans use these today but generally
they are connected with a heavy cable or chain for added security.

In the design and engineering of these anchored, stout posts,

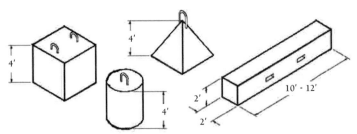

Concrete bollards can be made in a variety of shapes and sizes using such materials as plastic barrels or plywood for the forms. Make sure to coat the inner surface of the form liberally with oil to allow the concrete to release.

These plywood forms will make fine dragon's teeth.

the U.S. Department of State (DOS) developed a rating system for determining the most effective post for the expected threat. It has been adopted by other agencies and commercial users as well. Without getting into too much detail about the testing procedures, we can still benefit from the information. The K rating is now applied to all obstacles and structures that are to be used as anti-ramming devices or barriers.

The rating standards are as follows:

- K-4 rated bollards/barriers will stop a 15,000-pound vehicle traveling at 30 mph.
- K-8 rated bollards/barriers will stop a 15,000-pound vehicle traveling at 40 mph.
- K-12 rated bollards/barriers will stop a 15,000-pound vehicle traveling at 50 mph.

Note: The maximum allowed penetration into the protected area in all ratings above is 3 feet.

JERSEY BARRIER

Perhaps the best known and most feared of all the bollard-type barriers known to preppers today is the worrisome Jersey barrier.

While not practical for everyone to handle due to its size and weight, the Jersey barrier can also be a great improvement to the home retreat. Whether anchored to the ground or not, it has been proven from coast to coast to be able to stop cars and trucks dead in their tracks.

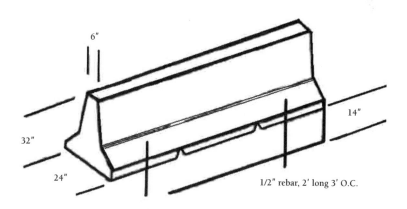

When anchored to a concrete slab (with driven rebar), the Jersey barrier has stopped a 4,000-pound vehicle traveling at 50 mph.

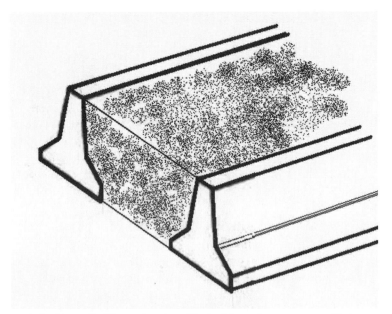

A double wall of Jersey barriers filled with earth or stone would stop nearly any vehicular threat that one could expect at a home retreat.

BOLLARD CONSTRUCTION

Building bollards to DOS standards can be expensive. Thankfully, there are less expensive options we can put in place, as well as alternatives in construction.

One of the most effective steel bollards is a steel I-beam driven into the ground and then covered with a steel pipe sleeve. Only the homeowner would realize the hidden strength beneath the pipe sleeve.

For those who have the resources to install steel pipe bollards at the retreat, consider the following chart that examines bollards and their performance. Note that all posts were set in concrete as tested.

Amount of Pipe Buried	Pipe Diameter	Height of Pipe above Ground	Crash Rating
24"	6 5/8"	30"	2,430 lbs @ 40 mph
24"	6 5/8"	36"	2,430 lbs @ 40 mph
36"	6"	30"	15,000 lbs @ 30 mph
36"	6"	36"	15,000 lbs @ 30 mph
36"	8"	30"	15,000 lbs @ 30 mph
36"	8"	36"	15,000 lbs @ 30 mph
36"	10"	36"	15,000 lbs @ 40 mph
36"	10"	36"	15,000 lbs @ 50 mph

It should also be noted that dirt packs harder in some areas of the world than it will in others. In the chirt and clay areas of the south, the dirt can be packed hard enough so that concrete may not be needed. Sandy or loam soils will need a greater mass of concrete to be fully effective. Extra time with the tamping iron end of a digging bar will pay off.

While they have not been tested under scientific controls and parameters, using a heavy, wood log as a bollard can also be an effective and less costly alternative. We have all seen what a large tree can do to a car traveling at high speeds along the highway. Using a large diameter post buried 3 or 4 feet in the ground or in concrete is an acceptable alternative. For many preppers, raiding the wood lot for stout log posts will be the most economical choice for bollards. Be sure to choose solid, fresh-cut timbers as large in diameter as you can handle (at least 10 inches). Hardwoods will be stronger than soft-wood trees or pine.

Used tires can be used as a bollard or vehicle obstacle. Check with the local tire dealer for his cast-offs, especially the heavy equipment tires. Half bury the tires, filling the inside with rocks and dirt and tamp until the ground is hard, or set it all in concrete.

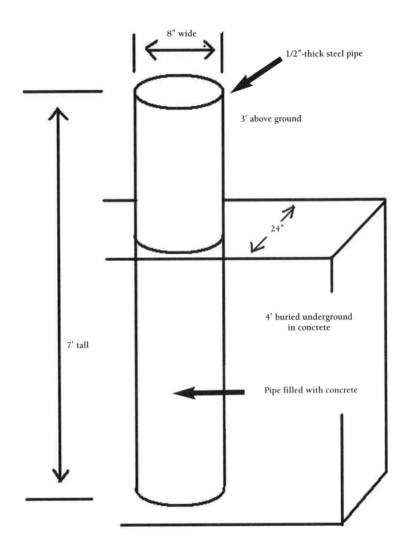

8" wide

1/2"-thick steel pipe

3' above ground

24"

4' buried underground in concrete

7' tall

Pipe filled with concrete

A bollard built to similar specifications was tested and found capable of stopping a 4,500-pound vehicle traveling at 30 mph. A similar post of 10 3/4-inches diameter tested to the K4 rating; a post of 12 3/4-inches diameter tested to the K12 rating. When using multiple posts, space them no more than 48 inches on center in steel-reinforced concrete.

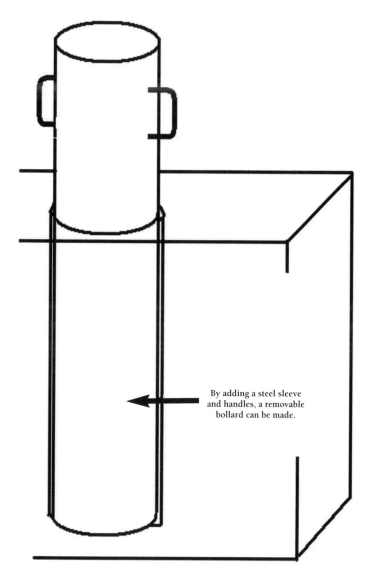

By adding a steel sleeve and handles, a removable bollard can be made.

Handles set into this bollard allow it to be moved to another location as needed.

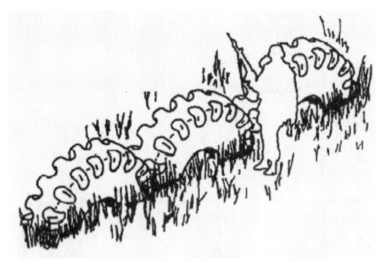

Heavy equipment tires, half buried, have been tested to
stop a 3,350-pound vehicle traveling at 50 mph.

BOLLARDS FOR SPEED CONTROL

The most effective use of this information for the home retreat relates to controlling the maximum speed that vehicles can
attain as they approach your barrier. In order to effectively protect your retreat, you must be able to control the attainable speed
of vehicles entering your property at all locations.

The speed of vehicles approaching your position can be controlled by sharp curves, tire-damaging devices, potholes, speed
bumps, and the type and depth of the gravel used on your driveway. Speed can also be controlled by cutting your driveway through
a heavily-wooded area using curves and trees to keep speeds low.

Lining your driveway with large boulders or rocks at the
break in a curve will serve to slow down vehicles by not allowing
them to stray from the road itself. Additionally, keeping the road-
way flat without banking the turns will contribute to keeping
vehicles from obtaining adequate ramming speeds. A steep-sided
short berm could also serve to slow down a vehicle or cause it to
lose control. This, too, is an acceptable stop. Large bushes and

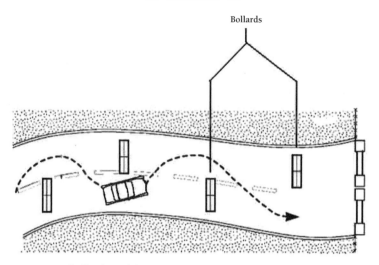

Keeping bollards and barriers closer together will inhibit a vehicle's attainable speed. Keep your road narrow and bollards close.

many types of shrubs planted to form a hedgerow can also be an effective barrier along your driveway. Discarded refrigerators, freezers, and even old cars can be used as bollards or barriers to slow the speed of an approaching threat.

By controlling the maximum speed a car or truck can obtain as it attempts to race up your driveway, you can be saving money as well. By keeping the attainable speed of the threat down, the use of smaller and lighter weight bollards can be employed. This is not a suggestion to go with lightweight materials, but rather to use an inexpensive tactic (speed control) to allow yourself to save money on materials.

THE CONCRETE GARDEN WALL

For the prepper who has the funds and skills (or friends who do), there can be no better bollard to have at the retreat than the concrete planter box. Not only is it an attractive addition to your retreat, but it also serves as a retaining wall barrier. A full fence, of sorts, surrounding your yard will give you an elevated, concrete planter box for your tomatoes while protecting your retreat

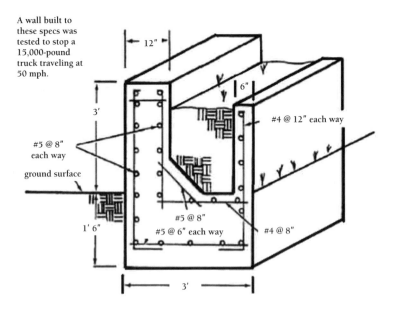

A wall built to these specs was tested to stop a 15,000-pound truck traveling at 50 mph.

12"

6"

3'

#4 @ 12" each way

#5 @ 8" each way

ground surface

1' 6"

#5 @ 8"
#5 @ 6" each way

#4 @ 8"

3'

Each wall must be calculated based on soil conditions at that site. Concrete strength = 3,000 psi. Reinforcement steel bars: fy = ksi. 1 1/2 inch concrete cover all around, except as noted. Source: Military FM 5-114

from an attack by a 15,000-pound vehicle traveling at 50 mph. What more could you want?

It should be mentioned that while the specs suggest 3,000 psi concrete, I would recommend ordering 4,000 psi or greater, if available. Concrete just reaches the threshold of being waterproof at 4,000 psi. The 3,000 psi concrete will absorb the water from your garden and it will freeze in the winter, slowly breaking apart your planter box.

The harder concrete makes for a more bulletproof barrier, as well. With 12 inches of primary concrete wall, even the .50 BMG will have a difficult time defeating your planter box.

For those who can afford this barrier, it should serve you well.

Once you start looking for them, you'll notice architectural security measures everywhere. The most obvious will be the post-style bollards, but there are many others that can be used at your home, too. The concrete planter box is just one of them. Any row of large concrete or steel objects placed close enough together so as to not allow a motor vehicle through will serve your purpose. String them together with chains and barbed wire to further slow down the advancing vehicular threat.

Half-buried refrigerators, cars, drums filled with concrete — whatever else your backyard junk pile can provide — may not be as attractive, but they will also work.

It is important to remember that our Department of State expects to see threats by suicidal fanatics driving car and truck bombs and has therefore engineered bollards to protect our embassies from these threats. This will most likely *not* be the threat the average prepper expects to encounter at the home retreat. Further, the domestic threat in a post-collapse world will most likely not include an attacker whose plan includes the loss of his escape vehicle. The level to which you fortify your home retreat should reflect the level of the expected threat. Of course, some sophisticated attackers may indeed have a throwaway vehicle included in their plans.

Chapter Five

Gabions

•

A gabion is a large cage or basket filled with earth that can be used in building or abutments. It comes from the Old Italian, "gabbione," which translates to "large cage." The first known use was in 1573.

More recently, during the American Revolution, it was common for gabions to be used at forts and semi-permanent gun positions. These gabions were hand-woven cages made on site from cut saplings or willow branches found in nearby forests, positioned and filled with the local dirt and stones. They allowed for earthen walls to surround a cannon and offered cover from small arms fire. Soon, woven, bottomless baskets were commissioned for the war effort.

The use of gabions on the battlefield has continued through all conflicts. During WWI, the hand-woven baskets that artillery shells were delivered in saw a second life as gabions protecting the artillery position.

Gabions are used in combat zones today as protective cover in fighting positions and bunkers worldwide. If you can't dig into the earth, you should still find a way to keep yourself surrounded by it. Gabions are for just that: stacking earth around your position.

They can be open to the ground below or caged at the bot-

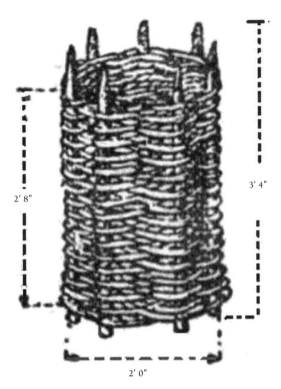

An early design and size for the gabion.

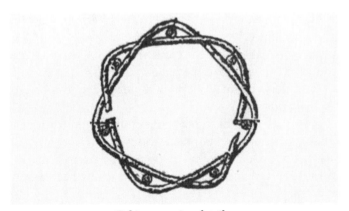

Gabion weaving detail.

Woven gabions like these provide heavy-duty stopping power.

tom when used elevated off the ground. Modern variations use crushed stone and a fabric liner to allow water to flow out but keep the stone inside the cage.

For the survivalist who was paying attention in Basket Weaving 101, old-style gabions should be an easy addition to the retreat.

A costlier but more effective gabion can be made on site from materials readily obtainable from the local farm store or big box building supply. Galvanized welded wire panels, commonly called hog fence, can be used to make a modern gabion at a relatively low cost. The biggest difference is the size of the squares in the mesh of the wire; hog panels have a larger square mesh than other types of mesh, but it is also a heavier-gauged wire.

Hog panels are typically sold in 16-foot lengths. You'll need a pair of bolt cutters and some erosion or sediment control cloth, along with a roll of heavy tie-wire or barb-less barbed wire (really, you can get this) and light-gauge tie wire. Since the hog panel squares are a bit too large, you'll also need a roll of cheap, lighter weight mesh, such as chicken wire.

These modern gabions are made from sections of hog fence.

Here's what to do:

Cut the hog panel into four equal lengths and turn them with the cut ends up and down so that the hard wire sides can be tied together with the heavy tie wire to form a box that's open on the top and bottom. Square the hog wire box and line it on the inside with the sediment control cloth. Use some of the light gauge tie wire to hold the cloth to the hog fence, keeping it in place.

Line the inside of the sediment cloth with the chicken wire using the light gauge tie wire to hold it in place as well. Use the heavy tie wire as wall supports by tying several strands centered, from wall to wall, in a crisscross fashion to keep the walls from bowing out when you add the crushed stone. Make as many wire

Photo: The Army Heritage Trail at the U.S. Army Heritage and Education Center.

Modern gabions filled with stone form a wall.

gabions as you need, and position them on a level surface where you want.

Carefully fill the hog fence gabions with crushed stone from your local quarry. Usually what is called crusher-run is the least expensive crushed stone to purchase.

You can experiment with lighter, less expensive wire meshes to save costs. Supporting the center of the cage walls from bending out from the weight of the stone is what's important. You can also fill your homemade gabions with your own local earth, stones, or rock. Additionally they can be placed in rows and stacked to make fortified structures.

Gabions are another excellent means for protective cover at the survival retreat.

Chapter Six

Revetments

•

A revetment is, simply, a protective wall. It can be made of wood, metal, concrete, or rock, but it always protects or supports something. Its first known use was in 1779.

The most commonly seen revetments often go unnoticed today. Landscaping timbers, used railroad ties, and decorative concrete blocks are used nearly everywhere as retaining walls to keep hills from sliding, on river and lake edges, and to define areas. Riprap stones protecting the shoreline from the surf are a type of revetment. Revetments are also what we call the wooden or steel fence-like shields at the end of runways to protect common areas from jet blast.

The military has been using protective walls since the beginning of time. Any wall you can build in the field that offers protection to you, your house, cars or trucks, or even just to protect a secure open area, is a revetment.

They are an additional choice for use at the home retreat as protective cover or to shore up a trench wall. As with any improvement to your home retreat, do a quick study of what you need protection from and study the lay of your land for what will work for you.

Common revetments used for protection from attack include large fabricated boxes similar in shape and design to the modern

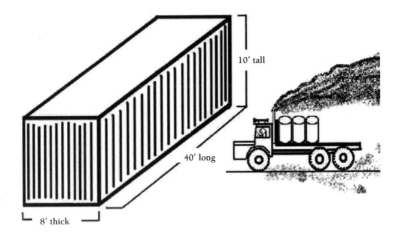

A 15,000-pound truck traveling at 50 mph is no
match for the mass of this K-12 rated revetment.

gabion (which is also a revetment). The difference is that they are
made from corrugated metal or plywood, not woven saplings.
Some commercially available revetments have been tested to
State Department Standards and have a K-rating for anti-ramming. These revetments are used as high-security fences that are
virtually ram-proof.

To give an illustration of how large a corrugated steel revetment would have to be to earn a DOS, K-12 rating, imagine a
metal-framed box with an exterior skin of corrugated metal roofing material. The box is open to the ground and will be later covered on top to keep the rain out. The box is 8 feet thick (wide),
10 feet tall, and 40 feet long. The box is filled with sand and dirt
to the top, compacted and leveled off, and a corrugated metal
roof is attached.

The protection offered by a dirt-filled box this size is enough
to defend against a Chevy C70 light-duty truck (15,000 pounds)
driven at 50 mph at a 90-degree angle right smack into the wall.
The end result would be that the truck's occupants would be
dead and the truck's cab completely destroyed, having been
crushed by the impact into the superior mass of the wall.

A revetment such as this would also deflect the blast wave of an explosion, offer excellent protection from close-range blasts, and absorb lethal shrapnel.

I can only guess what it would cost for the average prepper to fabricate boxes of this size. I think it would be in the neighborhood of too much. (Anyone with a few extra shipping containers could easily modify the roof, weld the doors shut, and use them for this purpose. They are very close in size and should perform similarly.)

Regardless of the potential cost, from a planning standpoint it is important to know how much earth-mass is needed to entirely stop an attack by a speeding truck headed right at you. From the test results reviewed, it's clear that you should go with a minimum of 8 feet of earth. Basic physics tells us that it was the total mass of the tested revetment that gave the end results and that the 10-foot height was a major contributing factor to the total mass. A wider revetment could have been shorter and given the same results.

Since the approximate ground to top-of-the-bumper (frame) measurement of a C70 truck (or similarly sized truck) is about 3 feet, an excavated earthen wall (near vertical) 3 feet in height with the earth mass at the same or greater height (behind the cut) would serve the same purpose, and when hit at 50 mph will likely see the occupants actually fly through the air. However, at approximately 3 feet high, this revetment could also be used against you by providing cover for an attacking force.

Constructing a wall to 6 feet or higher would help prevent it from being used against you. It should be placed either far enough away or close enough to be useless as effective cover for the threat. Additional deterrents such as barbed wire can also be used to keep a ground force out.

A properly placed excavated cut in your yard can be as effective as a military-grade revetment costing hundreds of thousands of dollars. Just remember: the greater the mass of the revetment, the greater the protection it provides.

Of course, your excavated wall may need a retaining wall revetment in order to keep it from eroding or collapsing.

Depending on the angle of approach, building your revetment a foot or two higher than the earthen side, thus concealing the mass of your barrier, could result in an uninformed attacker trying to ram through your wall — with disastrous results for him.

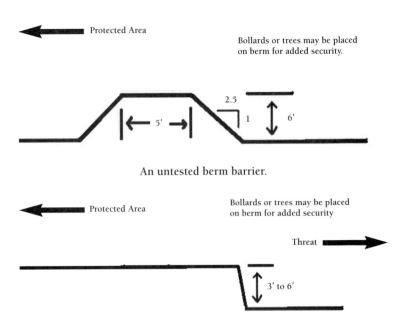

An untested berm barrier.

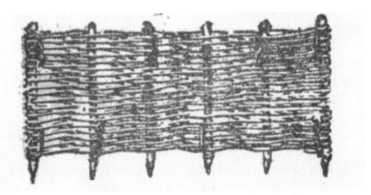

The better barrier. Add a brushwood revetment to hold up the excavated cut.

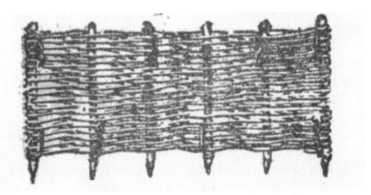

Hand-woven brushwood revetment panel, or hurdle.

What has been called the "brushwood hurdle" is more suitable for use as a revetment wall either above or below the surface in ditches or trenches.

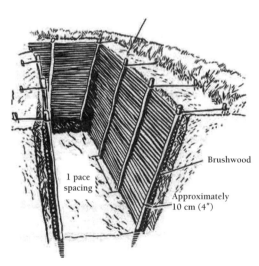

Continuous brushwood revetment used in a trench.

A hand-woven hurdle can be an inexpensive and attractive wall panel to use as a retaining wall revetment. Some more expensive alternatives would be landscaping timbers, railroad ties, or architectural landscape blocks.

Railroad ties and heavy log revetments serve as a retaining wall.

Modern landscaping blocks can be used around the home retreat
to make protective cover and stop vehicle ramming threats.

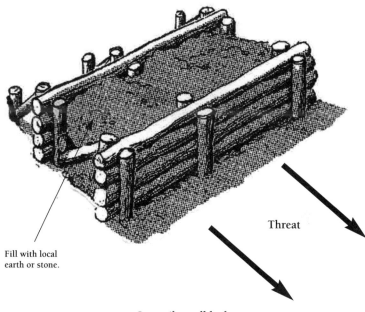

Fill with local
earth or stone.

Threat

Log crib roadblock.

Even when you lack the funds for steel and wire, effective revetments and deterrents can be made from materials found on your wood lot. Felling trees and building log cribs at various locations, the prepper can create a protective, cheap revetment or even roadblocks to slow approaching traffic.

Chapter Seven

Fascine

•

Fascine is an Old-World word that has a long history in warfare. It is a French word meaning "captive" or "captivated." Applied for our use, it is a captive bundle of sticks, branches, or small trees used to secure an embankment. It is really just another word for a revetment or a type of retaining wall material.

Using locally available trees or branches, bundles are tied together with wire or vines and staked into the ground to keep the side wall of a berm or a cut in place. The use of fascines can be another low-cost alternative for the home retreat.

It is of note that, during WWI and WWII, fascines were often carried by tanks and other vehicles to be used as a bridging material. The large bundles of small trees cut to a uniform length (wider than the vehicle that carried it) were dropped into a trench or small stream, and then they were driven over. This allowed vehicles to defeat a trench or stream that would have otherwise stopped the vehicle. Be alert to any vehicles approaching your defensive trenches or barrier streams and carrying fascines on their hoods or roofs.

Bundled branches and logs form a towering fascine.

Chapter Eight

Deliberate Defensive Fighting Positions

•

Most homes today are built of lightweight materials that could never hold up to a small arms skirmish, let alone a direct assault. It is often reported in the news that a stray bullet has either killed or wounded an innocent person while they were in their home. Few homes offer any level of protection against an armed assault, and almost none offer protective cover for deploying an adequate defense. For this reason, one or more deliberate fighting positions must be included in your home retreat plans.

There are several ways to increase the chances of surviving an assault on your home retreat long enough to rally defensive actions to end the threat. Body armor and helmets are highly recommended for everyone at your home retreat. Commercial or military-grade gas masks are also recommended, but neither the armor nor gas masks will give you enough continuous protection to allow you to take a stand against the attackers. Ballistic fiberglass panels can be installed in your walls and roof; however, these are expensive and only offer protection from small arms up to .44 caliber, not high-powered rifles.

The simplest deliberate positions are dug at select locations around the perimeter of your retreat. They can be one- or two-man positions and be covered or left uncovered. The first consideration for choosing a location to place any deliberate position should be its vantage point for observing an attacking force. Other considerations include how well it can be concealed from an attacking force and what areas a shooter or shooters will be able to cover with fire.

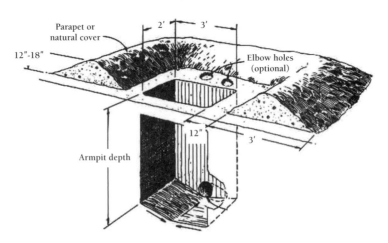

This is a one-man deliberate defensive position with a grenade sump at the center of a sloping floor. Take the time to set up a comfortable shooting position for threats coming from all expected directions.

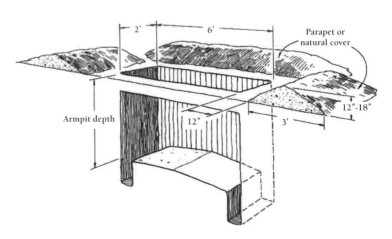

In a two-man deliberate position, put grenade sumps at each end of the sloping floor leading to a pit. Use soil to build a berm or parapet around the position.

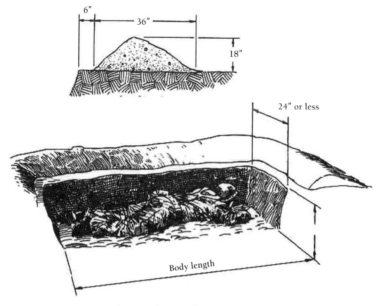

A typical prone hasty position.

Whenever possible, even when only one man is assigned to cover a defensive position, a two-man position should be built. Having the ability to adapt to the changing situation of an engagement can make the difference in a successful defense of your home. A fellow member of your retreat may have to join you, or you may have to cover two fields of fire from one position to make up a deficiency in your defense. In any event, be sure your back has some protective cover from each shooting position in your hole.

CONCEALING YOUR POSITION

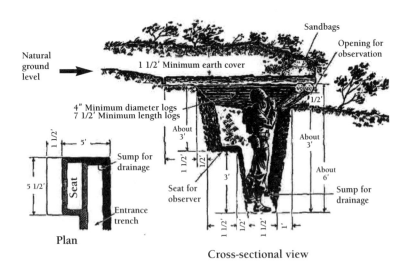

A covered and hidden observation outpost.

Overhead supports toward the front of the position need to be high
enough so as not to interfere with your line of sight or ability to shoot.

Overhead supports at rear can be lower.

Roofing logs can be 4 to 6 inches in diameter and should overhang the front and rear supports by about 6 inches. These will not be carrying a load of more than 12 to 18 inches of earth.

A waterproof roof will keep mud from seeping through and raining down on you while at your post. Use scrap plastic, trash bags, old ponchos, or plastic sheeting to add a waterproof layer over the logs.

Proper camouflage needs to be added using earth and foliage to conceal the position from all angles. In an urban environment, artificial items can be more liberally used if the surrounding area looks similar.

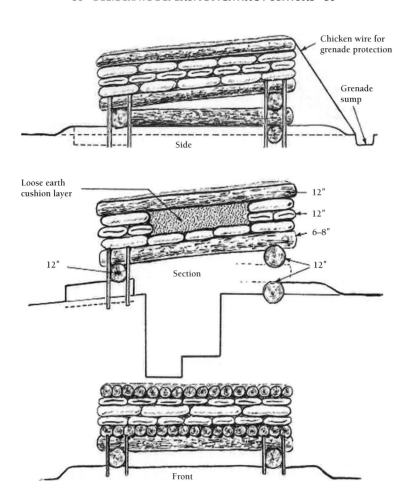

Fighting bunker with overhead cover.

THE HALF-PIPE BUNKER/SHELTER

Full and half-pipe bunkers and shelters have been used by the military since the invention of corrugated metal. The once-famous Quonset hut was perhaps the first widely recognized use of a radius-engineered metal building. It is still popular today and is offered by several metal-building suppliers throughout the United States.

If you have the funds to order such a building, by specifying that your building will be used in the heaviest of snow load areas, you'll get a building that is rated for pressures that would allow it to be fully buried with a few simple modifications. By keeping the length of the building down, or adding interior load-bearing bulkhead walls and capping the ends with solid concrete block or poured concrete walls, you will increase the load-bearing capacity of the structure.

There are several bomb shelters that are designed using lengths of corrugated metal pipe and are commercially available as well.

For those of us who don't have the funds to purchase and build these larger engineered structures, there are still affordable alternatives. Construction sites, highway construction yards, and scrap yards are great places to start looking for the right materials to make hardened structures for around the home retreat. The ideal size for the half-pipe shelter is a 5- or 6-foot radius pipe.

Corrugated metal pipe can be adapted for bunker construction.

These can be found as leftover materials or scraps from large highway and municipal projects. The contractors will sometimes even pay you to remove the items from the finished site.

If you can't find a pipe half, you can cut a full pipe in half lengthwise to double your materials. Collect a dozen or more steel, 55-gallon barrels and spring for some sandbags to make a half-pipe bunker/shelter.

A half-pipe bunker/shelter on the Army Heritage Trail at the U.S. Army Heritage and Education Center.

Steel 55-gallon barrels are used to create a shelter at the U.S. Army Heritage and Education Center.

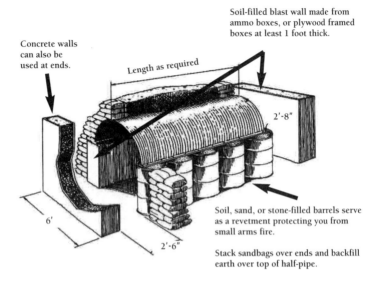

Soil-filled blast wall made from ammo boxes, or plywood framed boxes at least 1 foot thick.

Concrete walls can also be used at ends.

Length as required

2'-8"

6'

2'-6"

Soil, sand, or stone-filled barrels serve as a revetment protecting you from small arms fire.

Stack sandbags over ends and backfill earth over top of half-pipe.

The half-pipe metal culvert pipe bunker/shelter.

The half-pipe corrugated metal top must be secured to the top of the sidewalls; otherwise, the sides will spread and the top will collapse under the weight of the sandbags and earth.

To secure the sidewalls of the half-pipe to the top of a formed and poured concrete sidewall, use standard 1/2-inch anchor bolts set in the top of the concrete. Bolt a 2x8 board to the bottom of the half-pipe flange using framing anchors, and bolt the 2x8 to the top of the concrete wall at the anchor bolts.

To secure the half-pipe sidewalls to an earth-filled 55-gallon drum, measure and cut 2x4 posts to sit inside at the center of the barrels *before* you fill them with dirt. The 2x4s should be about 4 inches taller than the barrels and run parallel with the sides of the culvert pipe edge. Keep the 4x4s lined up straight as you fill the barrels, and then fasten the 2x8 side rails to the tops of the 2x4s. The same structure can be built using corrugated plastic drainpipe as well.

Another item to keep watch for while salvaging building materials is a section of large concrete sewer pipe 48 inches in diam-

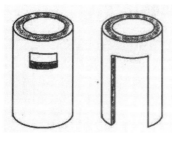

Concrete sewer pipe defensive shelters.

eter or larger. These are usually very heavy and will not be easily moved by most preppers. It will require a very heavy-duty flatbed trailer along with a 1-ton or larger truck to tow it. Further, it will require a backhoe or other piece of heavy equipment to properly set up. This being said, if you can handle this type of job the reward can be great.

Pre-cast concrete sewer pipes are made of very high-pressure, reinforced concrete and made to last. They are also bulletproof. My own nonscientific tests on reinforced, high-pressure (7,000 psi) concrete 2 inches thick showed that the concrete deflected small arms fire up to a .308 Winchester with little damage to the concrete.

Obtaining 7,000 psi concrete is not easy to achieve in a field operation, but most precast concrete plants routinely achieve this level and higher in order to meet necessary standards. This is why certain concrete building materials, such as sewer pipes that must be waterproof, are made in precast concrete factories instead of being poured at the job site.

By turning one of these pipes up on its end and cutting out a doorway and a shooting porthole, you have an excellent defensive shelter. Properly placed, a man stationed inside would have a great advantage over an armed attacker. By stacking two or more sections of the concrete pipe, an elevated, protected observation tower can be made.

After the concrete pipe gets placed in position, use a concrete cut saw to cut out the doorway and gun port. Corrugated metal roofing can be cut to size and used to pour a concrete top to your bulletproof shelter. Two such shelters placed 12 feet apart at your retreat's entrance make very nice gateposts. With a little more planning, they can be placed on a poured concrete pad and permanently set.

THE METAL DRUM

There are endless uses for 55-gallon drums at the home retreat. Aside from the standard uses of storing oils and fuels, metal drums make excellent gabion alternatives for cover from gunfire. If you can gather enough, they can be used as protective cover around the perimeter of your non-hardened buildings. Barns, cabins, outhouses, or any other retreat structure that might require protection from gunfire can be surrounded with filled barrels of earth.

In a similar manner, crates and ammo boxes can be filled with earth or crushed stone to create protective cover from gunfire.

When placed approximately 4 feet off the structure, the barrels offer immediate cover from gunfire to those who exit the building or continuous cover to those inside at floor level.

The barrels surrounding this cabin demonstrate excellent cover from gunfire. Without the added protective cover, this cabin would provide no protection in a skirmish.

Crates and ammo boxes filled with earth or crushed
stone can create good cover from gunfire.

Photo: The Army Heritage Trail at the U.S. Army Heritage and Education Center.

SANDBAGS

Most preppers are familiar with the multiple uses of sandbags. They are relatively inexpensive (between 8 and 35 cents
each at this writing) and can be deployed quickly when you have
a lot of willing and able help. The standard size for sandbags is
16 inches by 27 inches when empty. This allows 160 bags, properly filled to three-quarters full and single stacked, to cover a
revetment of 100 square feet. A double-stacked and interlocked
wall would use about 320 bags.

The biggest drawback of poly sandbags when used at the
home retreat is their lack of longevity. Left out in the open, they
will start to break apart from the effects of UV light in about
1,600 daylight hours, or approximately six months.

For this reason, the prepper should be ready to cover the
sandbags with a waterproof layer of plastic sheathing and add a
layer of earth covering the sheathing as well. Burlap sandbags
can last even less time when exposed to the elements.

It's easy for the tired and weary to lose their focus when stacking sandbags, but certain rules must be followed to ensure your sandbag wall or revetment doesn't fall in on you at an inopportune moment.

- Interlocking the rows and columns of your sandbag stacks is a *must*.
- Keep the folded ends and seamed side of the bags to the inside of the wall stack and away from the foot traffic that might catch it and break a bag open.
- Try to keep your placed sandbags similar in size and shape. Don't overfill them.

To aid the willing and able with the labor-intensive task of filling the sandbags, a chute can be constructed that can greatly cut down on the time required.

Correct placement of sandbags with joints of the stacks broken.

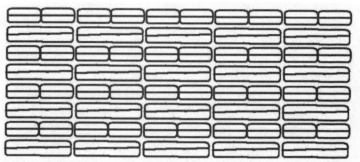

While it does look nice and neat, this is the wrong way to stack sandbags.

A sturdy wooden chute such as this one can
make filling sandbags a little easier.

Additionally, there is a new product available that greatly
reduces the amount of time it takes to fill sandbags and even
makes filling sandbags a one-man operation. The GoBagger is a
handheld scooper available for around $60 through supply
houses and online.

Sandbags have long been recognized as an excellent protective option when used in the construction of both revetments
and breastworks in fortifying a retreat. Breastworks are just what
they sound like: a sandbag wall approximately breast high. They

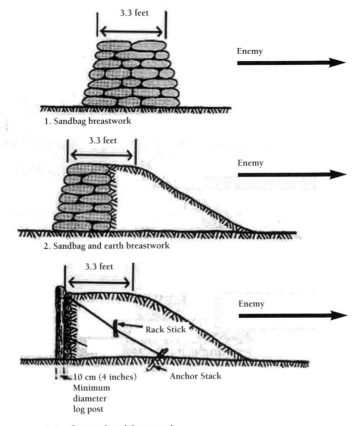

1. Sandbag breastwork

2. Sandbag and earth breastwork

3. Log fence and earth breastwork

**Sandbags and earthworks must be more than
3 feet thick to offer protective cover.**

are used in especially wet areas where digging a trench would be impossible due to a high water table.

THE WOOD-FRAMED FIGHTING POSITION

The wood-framed fighting position is perhaps the best choice for the defense of your home retreat. It is easy to build and offers

The wood-framed fighting position has many advantages.

substantial protection. Once constructed, it is easily adaptable to whatever materials for protective cover you have available.

Heavy timbers and lumber are used to construct a stout wood-framed, covered structure that can support heavy loads of sand, earth, or rock. This structure offers the advantages of a hardened buried bunker but allows for a topside full view of the battlefield. Properly placed, a deliberate position such as this will allow for a strong defense of your home retreat.

It can be protected by bermed earth, gabions, revetments, or sandbags. With heavy beams carrying the roof load, it can also have an elevated shooting position. Additionally, when an extended overhang is used and the roof is covered with 90-pound rolled roofing, a bed of earth can be placed for grass and plants to be grown for excellent concealment from above. My wife wants to plant her vegetable garden here; from the air, it would look like a small garden plot.

A defensive position made from a wood-framed
fighting position and modern gabion barriers.

Note the heavy timber frames used to support the
weight of the earth and rock-filled gabion barriers.

Timber framework shown before
the addition of the gabion barriers.

Timber framework shown supporting sandbags.

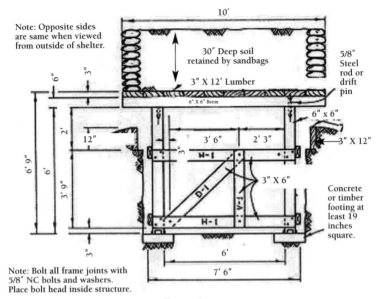

Note: Opposite sides are same when viewed from outside of shelter.

10'

30" Deep soil retained by sandbags

5/8" Steel rod or drift pin

3" X 12' Lumber

6" X 6" Beem

6" x 6"

3' 6"   2' 3"

3" X 12"

6' 9"   6'   3' 9"

12"

3"

W-1

3" X 6"

D-1

H-1

Concrete or timber footing at least 19 inches square.

3"

6'

7' 6"

Note: Bolt all frame joints with 5/8" NC bolts and washers. Place bolt head inside structure.

Front view

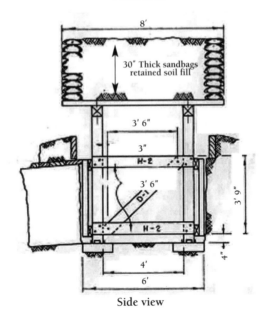

8'

30" Thick sandbags retained soil fill

3' 6"

3"

H-2

3' 6"

D-1

3' 9"

H-2

4"

4'

6'

Side view

Timber-framed fighting position.

Chapter Nine

Trenches
and
Tunnels

•

Now that you have plans for obstacles, bunkers, and fighting positions for your retreat, you need a way to get in and out and a safe path between them all. Don't be trapped in your own deliberate position. The time to think about an escape route is now, before you actually fortify anything.

A crawl trench may be the least expensive pathway that provides safe cover from gunfire, costing only your labor or a backhoe rental. Crawl trenches can get you under barbed-wire entanglements and fences, as well as open fields. They may offer cover from fire when moving from structure to structure on the retreat. Wherever the vantage point for line-of-sight observation by the enemy is too low to see the trench or too far to get off an accurate shot, a crawl trench can prove to be an effective tool.

Longer crawl trenches will require extra attention as to their observability. It may be necessary to zigzag or include several turns in the path to ensure the intruders cannot get a good view of your movement. The used dirt, or spoil, from trenches dug inside your compound can be used as a berm on the protective side of the trench without added concern. It is a given that the enemy knows you will be moving inside your own compound; you just don't want them to be able to see your movements.

Inexpensive to make, the crawl trench provides safe cover from fire.

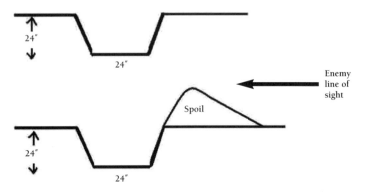

Adding a berm of spoil adds to the concealment power of your trench.

However, crawl trenches used as an escape route from your compound need to be well concealed and camouflaged from the intruders. The spoil needs to be either removed completely or used in such a manner that the enemy cannot see your escape path from any outside vantage point. If an intruder is able to see your escape route, you can count on being ambushed on your way out.

Tunnels are more costly to construct but offer the ultimate in concealment. They can also be virtually any size that allows you to move through them. Advanced Drainage Systems manufactures several types of flexible plastic drainpipe in various sizes, from one that would allow a man to crawl through to sizes large enough to walk upright.

Using a flexible plastic drainpipe or even a metal culvert pipe with a diameter of 30 inches, a well-concealed escape tunnel can be placed completely out of the enemy's sight. The outside opening of the tunnel would be your biggest concern.

But be aware that these tunnels are a two-way street; culvert pipes large enough to allow you to crawl through and escape can also allow the intruder to crawl through to you. And even if your culvert escape pipe is disguised as a drainpipe, it will undoubtedly be noticed by the intruder and identified as a possible route to your inner compound.

All pipe and tunnel exits should be well hidden and concealed by natural foliage or require a short dig to daylight to complete your ultimate escape. It would be a good idea to keep a small shovel or entrenching tool at the end of the tunnel so you're not using your rifle to dig the final couple of feet during an escape.

As with any excavation, before starting your dig, carefully relocate any usable native plants or sod to be replaced later and used to camouflage any evidence of your digging. Once the plants have been put aside, scrape the top layer of mulch or soil to be used again later in returning the area to its former appearance. Time heals all wounds as far as digging goes, but we really don't know how much time we have.

The aerial photo of the men in foxholes shown on page 77 il-

DRAINAGE PIPE TUNNELS

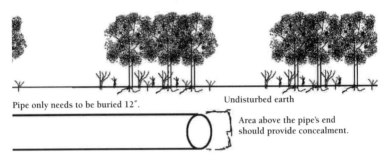

Pipe only needs to be buried 12″.

Undisturbed earth

Area above the pipe's end
should provide concealment.

Position the end of your pipe tunnel to take
advantage of existing foliage for concealment.

OPEN END DRAINAGE PIPE TUNNELS

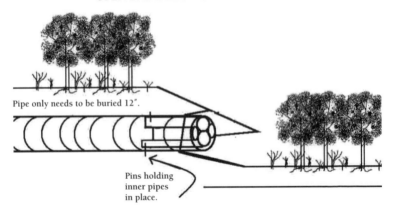

Pipe only needs to be buried 12″.

Pins holding
inner pipes
in place.

When using an open-end drainage pipe tunnel, plan to fill the crawl pipe
end with 4- to 5-foot lengths of smaller pipe to prevent entry by intruders.
Pin the inside ends of the smaller pipes to keep them in place. When
egress is needed, pull the pins and push the smaller pipes out.

These soldiers may have adequate concealment from ground forces, but they are not protected from air reconnaissance.

lustrates how important it is to conceal and camouflage your positions from all angles. In today's age of drones and satellite surveillance, it's best to keep your projects small and quick to avoid long-term opportunities for prying eyes to discover what you'd rather keep to yourself. If the project is large, try breaking it down into smaller, more manageably concealed projects where you can control the overhead exposure. Otherwise, you'll be spending a lot of money at the Army-Navy store on vast amounts of camo netting.

Brush or branches can be woven into wire fencing supported by wooden frames and then used as cover for one- or two-man positions (foxholes). Another inexpensive and lightweight cover for your smaller positions can be made by building a brushwood revetment hurdle and laying it over your foxhole.

Larger trenches can cost more to build but will allow you to move freely through the compound. Dug out and shored up with revetments and braces, a trench system can be a nice addition to a home retreat, especially if the group or family is large enough to fill all the perspective positions the system of trenches pro-

A large trench makes use
of revetments and braces.

Scrap wood from old pallets, often obtained
for free, can be used to line your trench.

Here you can see a trench with an elevated wooden floor
ending at a sandbagged bunker on a World War I battlefield.

Trenches always lead to bunkers.

vides. Concealment can be accomplished through the use of camouflage netting or by covering the top of the trench with plywood and rolled roofing and an inch or two of earth.

The best trench systems are designed with wood plank flooring placed several inches above the bottom of the excavation and wood plank walls. If you live anywhere it rains, you can bet an assault on your retreat will take place on the rainiest day of the year. Don't get caught by your own mud. Start collecting wooden pallets and fill in their open slots so you don't turn your ankle. Heavy timbers can be found at surplus railroad yards and landscape supply yards. Watch for highway improvement projects in your area. Often, they just want the old materials gone. Once, I was able to get hundreds of 8x8, 6-foot-long, creosote-treated timbers for $1 a piece.

Chapter Ten

Bunkers

•

Everyone I know wants a bunker. Even my wife wants a bunker. She just has a different name for it. She keeps calling it a root cellar. I'd even go so far to say that, if asked, *everyone* would want a bunker. Most of us want a full-fledged thermonuclear bomb bunker with electricity, running water, and room enough to store seven years of food and shelter our entire family. Just a modest bunker, but one with a secure door that we could shut, lock, and pretty much live behind without any worries. In fact, there are several well-engineered bunker/structure systems available for large groups and municipalities that just might meet these criteria. These bunker systems would be nice to have, but it happens that I'm coming up a little short on the cash needed to build one.

It is no surprise that people in America's tornado alley who have root cellars use them as storm shelters as well. Survivalists and preppers should be gardening, canning, and storing their foods in a root cellar in any event. Modifying your root cellar plans may provide all the storage and survival bunker you need. Placing a secondary root cellar at a remote or hidden location on your property might be a retreat-from-battle alternative, too.

For those like me without the funds to build the ultimate bunker, consider the alternatives. Bunkers can be complex or

A pillbox concrete bunker in Bulgaria.

simple; made of dirt, wood, or concrete; and be any size. They can be for food and material storage or just to protect a single person for a short time. A bunker can be both a protected fighting position and a hidden escape point. The question becomes, what can you afford and for what are you seeking safe storage or protection? Your first consideration should be to determine what the threat is.

THREAT ASSESSMENT

A threat assessment must be done to determine what level of fortification will adequately protect you. A thorough threat assessment takes time to conduct, but it starts with what you already believe to be true and is perhaps at the very core of your beliefs as a prepper. You have already identified the possibility of a threat and are getting prepared for an event or events that will bring the threat to your door.

The next step is to develop "Plan A." This is your default retreat; the place you believe that, under most circumstances, you will be able to defend and protect. It is where you are building a store of supplies to carry you through tough times. More than likely you already live there. Plan A is your home.

Wherever this location happens to be, you must conduct a survey of the greater surrounding area. Map out your location and accurately draw your home and the immediate neighbors' homes and outbuildings, along with all streets, alleys, and paths. Detail any and all fences that exist, describing how high they are and of what materials they are made.

Get to know your neighbors well enough to determine if they will be friend or foe in difficult times. Are they like-minded, or are they part of the problem? What would they bring to the table when the SHTF? Not all preppers are at the same level of preparedness. You may have a neighbor who is like-minded and with good intentions but unable to afford all that is needed. He may not bring 200 pounds of beans to the table, but he can shoot and owns a rifle and ammo. Without disclosing your situation, you should be able to decide if he would be a friend or foe.

In contrast, you may not know who lives two blocks over but, after spending a Saturday afternoon driving around the neighborhood, you discover a house that appears to be home to about 30 or 40 young adults, all foreign in appearance. Does it look like a well-organized prepper group, or is it a collection of national interlopers? Is it likely that this group is a threat? You may have to consider this as an unknown or a yet-to-be-determined threat. Make notations on your map with names and locations accordingly.

Conduct reconnaissance missions both on foot and in a vehicle to the extent necessary for you to know your surrounding area. While you are observing, you should make notes as to what safe paths you could take if you need to implement Plan B or bug out of your Plan A location. What path offers concealment? Is there any safe cover from gunfire enroute? Take your notes back to your location and put them on your map. Pay special attention to creeks and streams, as well as any hills, woods, and wide-open areas, making notations on your map as you go.

The Internet and Google Maps offer preppers an excellent opportunity to review their findings and keep their maps to scale. Distances can be plotted with reasonable accuracy between critical points.

Once you have mapped out your world, you can then ponder who will be coming and the routes they will take. As you review what types of groups might be visiting your location, it would be good to know what kind of assets they have. What kind of vehicles do they own? What is the largest and heaviest truck they have? Will they be a uniformed group of invaders, or will they be an unorganized mob from the next town over? Do they own off-road vehicles or four-wheelers? Do they own any horses? Are they hunters? Will they arrive by road or by jumping the backyard fence? Answering these questions will further help determine your fortification needs.

Another aspect to threat assessment is in deciding what of yours actually is worth protecting. Clearly, your food and water supply would need protection as well as your guns and ammo, but does your car or truck need to be protected? Is it your Plan B escape vehicle and do you have enough fuel to actually use it?

Caching supplies outside your determined perimeter for retrieval at a later time is also advisable. Bugging out will often mean leaving much behind.

It is highly recommended that you establish a warning system with trusted friends and like-minded individuals to alert each other in the event of an imminent threat. Further, it is also recommended that you determine what your actions will be before the threat occurs rather than just winging it.

Your plan of action should include both a retreat option and a stand option. There is no shame in running and living to fight another day. But standing against a superior force should only be done when there are no other options available or your level of fortification ensures your survival.

SAFETY GUIDELINES

Once you have determined what the expected threat is, you can begin to plan what type of bunker will best meet your protection needs. There are several elements to safety when dis-

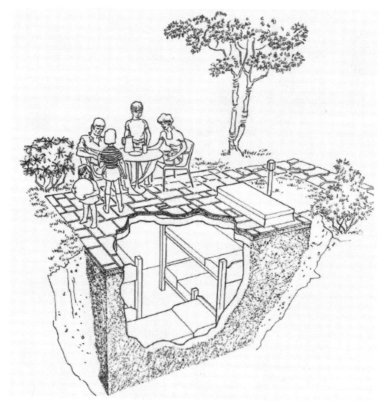

This quaint image of a 1950s-style fallout shelter bears
little resemblance to the realities of survival.

cussing and planning the construction of the bunker itself.
Whenever possible, use a tried-and-proven design to ensure you
don't fall victim to the collapse of your own project.

U.S. military field fortifications have been tested, tried, and
proven in the field. On the other hand, anyone who has studied
the Civil Defense or FEMA civilian shelters and bunkers should
notice right away that they are lacking in practical design and use
where fortification is concerned. Any fallout shelter that is covered with less than 3 feet of earth or its equivalent, and does not
include enough protected space to store food and fresh drinking
water, will simply ensure a slow death if put to the ultimate test.

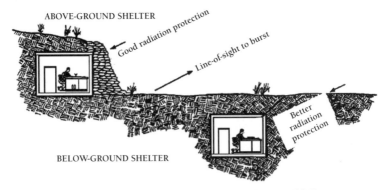

The most effective protection from both local and fallout radiation starts with 3 feet of earth as overhead shielding.

The fallout shelter illustration on the previous page might have been adequate by 1950s standards for an under-informed populace who trusted their government to be forthright, but it does not begin to meet the needs of today's survivor of a nuclear attack or direct assault.

Reviewing our military's radiation shelter minimums will give a better idea of what type of nuclear protection the survival retreat requires.

The following tables tell the story. They should be reviewed and used to determine what type of bunkers will serve your retreat the best (based on the threats you expect) and what materials to use when radiation is your concern.

Clearly, more earth over your head equals better protection from radiation. Having an underground bunker will also provide excellent blast protection, but you'd have to have advance warning before the event. Depending on the severity of a societal-economic collapse, early warning systems may not even be manned, let alone in working condition. Hopefully you'll be in the middle of organizing your bunker's shelves when the event occurs.

Surface shelters that are covered can also provide adequate protection from radiation but should have a blast-protective entrance in case your neighbors try to burn you out of your bunker with a flame-thrower. It would also serve to protect your entrance from direct exposure to bomb blasts.

INITIAL RADIATION EFFECTS ON PREPPERS
Early Symptoms*

Dose in Rads (cGy)	Percentage of Cases that Require Medical Attention	Time until Effect	Combat Effectiveness of Prepper	Fatalities
0-70	< 5% will be hospitalized		Full	None
150	5%	< 6 hours	Effectiveness reduced depending on task. Some hospitalized.	None
650	100%	< 2 hours	Symptoms continue intermittently for next few days. Effectiveness reduced significantly in second to sixth day. Hospitalization will be required.	50%-plus in about 16 days
2,000 to 3,000	100%	< 5 minutes	Immediate temporary incapacitation for 30–40 minutes, followed by recovery period during which efficiency is impaired. No operational capacity.	100% in about 7 days
8,000	100%	< 5 minutes	Immediate permanent incapacitation for those involved in physically demanding tasks. No period of latent recovery.	100% in 1–2 days
18,000	100%	Immediate	Permanent incapacitation for preppers performing undemanding tasks. No operational capability.	100% within 24 hours

* Symptoms include vomiting, diarrhea, dry heaving, nausea, lethargy, depression, and mental disorientation. At lower doses, incapacitation is a simple slowdown in performance rate due to a loss of physical mobility and/or mental disorientation. At the high-dose levels, shock and coma are sometimes the early symptoms.

SHIELDING VALUES OF EARTH COVER
AND SANDBAGS FOR A HYPOTHETICAL
2,400-RADS (CGY) FREE-IN-AIR DOSE

Type of Protection	Radiation Protection Factor	Resulting Dose Rads to Prepper
Prepper in the open	None	2,400 rads

Results for Earth-Covered Positions

Prepper in 4'-deep open position	8	300 rads
With:		
6" of earth cover	12	200 rads
12" of earth cover	24	100 rads
18" of earth cover	48	50 rads
24" of earth cover	96	25 rads

Results for Sandbag-Covered Positions (Clay or Sand-Filled)

Prepper in 4'-deep open position	8	300 rads
With:		
1 layer of sandbags (4")	16	150 rads
2 layers of sandbags (8")	32	75 rads
3 layers of sandbags (12")	64	38 rads

Aside from the threat of thermonuclear annihilation that looms over all of us, the prepper should also look at the effects of small arms and artillery rounds and at the established and proven protections bunkers afford against these weapons. It may prove costly to build every bunker to nuclear-war protection standards, but it may also be what saves your life.

The tables in this section are for those preppers who want to investigate bunkers that offer protection against attacks with conventional military weapons.

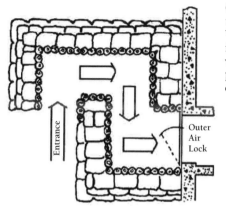

Overhead view of a blast-protected bunker entrance. Whether the assault is from a flamethrower or a nuclear device, this design will offer protection for the inhabitants of the bunker.

MATERIAL THICKNESS (IN INCHES) REQUIRED TO PROTECT AGAINST INDIRECT FIRE FRAGMENTATION AND BLAST EXPLODING 50 FEET AWAY

Material	Mortars 82mm	120mm	122mm Rocket	HE Shells 122m	152mm	100 lb	250 lb	Bombs 500 lb	1,000 lb
Solid Wall									
Brick masonry	4	6	6	6	8	8	10	13	17
Concrete	4	5	5	5	6	8	10	15	18
Concrete reinforced	3	4	4	4	5	7	9	12	15
Timber	8	12	12	12	14	15	18	24	30
Wall of Loose Material between Boards									
Brick rubble	9	12	12	12	12	18	24	28	30
Earth*	12	12	12	12	16	24	30	—	—
Gravel/small stones	9	12	12	12	12	18	24	28	30
Sandbags filled with:									
Brick rubble	10	18	18	18	20	20	20	30	40
Clay*	10	18	18	18	20	30	40	40	50
Soil	10	18	18	18	20	20	20	30	40
Sand*	8	16	16	16	18	30	30	40	40
Loose parapets of:									
Clay*	12	20	20	20	30	36	48	60	—
Sand*	10	18	18	18	24	24	36	36	48

* Double values if material is saturated.
Note: Where no value is given, material is not recommended.

CENTER-TO-CENTER SPACING FOR WOOD STRINGERS/BEAMS SUPPORTING EARTH COVER TO DEFEAT CONTACT BURST

Nominal Stringer Size (inches)	Depth of Dirt in Feet	Center-to-Center Stringer Spacing in Inches for Cited Span Length in Feet				
		2	4	6	8	10
For Defeat of a 82mm Contact Burst						
2x4	2	3	4	4	4	3
	3	18	12	8	5	3
	4	18	14	7	4	3
2x6	2	4	7	8	8	6
	3	18	18	16	12	8
	4	18	18	18	11	7
4x4	2	7	10	10	9	7
	3	18	18	18	12	8
	4	18	18	18	10	7
For Defeat of a 120mm/122mm Contact Burst						
4x8	1.5	4	5	7	8	8
	2	14	18	18	18	18
	3	18	18	18	18	18
6x6	4			5.5	6	6
	5	14	14	13	12	10
	6	18	18	18	16	12
6x8	4	5.5	6	8	9	10
	5	18	18	18	18	17
8x8	4	7.5	9	11	12	13
	5	18	18	18	18	18
For Defeat of a 152mm Contact Burst						
4x8	4					3.5
	5	6	6	7	7	7
	6	17	16	14	12	10
	7	18	18	18	15	11
6x6	5	7	8	8	8	7
	6	18	18	15	12	10
	7	18	18	18	15	11
6x8	4					6
	5	10	11	12	12	12
	6	18	18	18	18	17
8x8	4					8
	5	14	15	16	17	16
	6	18	18	18	18	18

See next page for Notes.

Note: Eighteen inches is the maximum beam spacing to preclude further designs. A top sheathing of wood or plywood should be placed over the stringers (maximum 1 inch) for 82mm direct bursts and 2 sheets of plywood used for 120- to 150mm bursts.

Due to the extreme depth the bunkers would need for this protection level, it is highly recommended that the roof supports be over the top of a secondary inner bunker structure and *not* a simple trench bunker.

Bunkers at this depth will also require positive airflow with proper fresh air ventilation.

It is worth pointing out that this level of contact burst protection can also offer a high level of protection from the effects of radiation but may not be the best fighting position.

MAXIMUM SPAN OF 2X4s AND 2X6s WHEN USED AS ROOF STRINGERS FOR THE SUPPORT OF EARTH-COVERED ROOFS

Thickness of Earth Cover in Feet	Span Length in Feet for 2x4s					
	2 1/2	3	3 1/2	4	5	6
	Center-to-Center Spacing of Stringers in Inches					
1 1/2	40	30	22	16	10	
2	33	22	16	12		
2 1/2	27	18	12	10		
3	22	14	10			
3 1/2	18	12	8			
4	16	10	8			

Thickness of Earth Cover in Feet	Span Length in Feet for 2x6s					
	2 1/2	3	3 1/2	4	5	6
	Center-to-Center Spacing of Stringers in Inches					
1 1/2						18
2					8	14
2 1/2					16	10
3				8	14	8
3 1/2			24	18	12	8
4			20	10	10	7

Note: Do not exceed these maximum spans, or thicknesses of earth, when building wooden-framed, underground shelter roofs. Going with heavier or larger stringer sizes is always preferable.

When considering your bunker's design and the materials you'll be using, it is clear that the more earth you have between you and the threat, the better off you'll be. Do an inspection of your ground. What type of soil do you have? Are there rocks available nearby? At what level is the water table?

It is important to keep your bunker's dirt dry. Water from rain or melting snow will not only help wash away all your hard work, but it will also seep into your earthen walls and cover, diminishing the effectiveness of the protection and adding unwanted excessive weight to your roof. Neither of these results is good.

A good illustration of the differences in protection afforded by wet vs. dry earth is to consider which one you'd rather be digging in. Digging is tough when the ground is dry, but water loosens the earth and the shovel will go deep. Now replace the shovel with a pointed, ballistic projectile or missile. The drier and harder the pack of earth or soil, the better it defends against attacks. Keep your earthen walls and roofs protected from the rains.

One of the best ways to block rain is to use the black plastic landscape rolls available at big box home improvement stores. Use the plastic as a cover before you place the last foot or less of dirt on your bunker or position. Be sure to completely bury or cover the plastic with dirt, rocks, or concealment because it can reflect light like a mirror in the sun and give your position away.

Each prepper, survivalist, or modern-day-apocalypse homesteader will have to decide for himself what level of protection he wants and can afford. Time is short, but there is still time to prepare.

BUILDING WITH LOGS

Preppers without the extra funds to be running to the lumberyard every two days to pick up dimensional lumber can still construct bunkers at their retreat. Having a wooded lot can be just like having a lumberyard. While a chainsaw will come in handy, a two-man crosscut saw will also work.

Make sure you don't cut trees that serve as barriers along your driveway or established security perimeter. You may also want to avoid taking all the trees from one location unless you have other plans for that spot. Make the most of your surroundings by harvesting your trees from an area that will be better without them, such as expected fields of fire or areas that provide you with a long-distance viewing point.

When choosing trees to harvest for your load-bearing spans, look for straight trees with at least 8 feet of trunk with little or no taper. Stay away from hollow trees or trees that are too large in diameter to handle by your crew of preppers.

This section contains a chart to help you calculate how to replace the load-bearing, dimensional lumber in your plans for logs from trees cut down on your land.

CONVERTING LOG SIZE
TO DIMENSIONAL LUMBER SIZE

Log Diameter in Inches	Structural Equivalent Dimensional Size
5	4x4
7	6x6
8	6x8
10	8x8
11	8x10
12	10x10
13	10x12
14	12x12

Note: Measure logs from the smaller diameter end, excluding the bark of the tree. Dimensional sizes given are nominal and not rough-cut timber sizes.
When determining what logs you can use, don't worry about over-engineering your bunker. Using an 8-inch diameter log (6x8 equivalent) where the minimum size called for is a 2x6 just means you have a bunker that is made better than the minimum standards. Stay away from soft or old dead trees. Only use fresh-cut hardwoods with clear straight runs and no rot whenever possible. Soft woods like pine should only be used when there is no alternative and where the loads are light.

THE REMOTE BUNKER

Not having ample funds for every security measure available should not be considered a disadvantage. In today's hi-tech world of threat detection and military hardware, the simplest wood-frame and earth structures at remote locations, properly placed, known only by you and accessible only by foot, stand the best chance of never being detected.

The first security measure that must be followed is to keep your mouth shut. Tell no one about your plans. "Loose lips sink ships," for sure. The only people involved in the construction of the remote bunker should be the actual users. Materials might be picked up and purchased with cash from out-of-town suppliers. It is not uncommon for the code enforcement police to follow homeowner's trucks, loaded with materials, home from the local lumberyard to check for permits. Know your area and what precautions to take to ensure your secret is kept.

Satellite imagery, however, can detect the signs that will give your position away, if not your bunker itself. If your project is to be a remote bunker located away from your home or primary retreat and accessible only on foot, it is best to follow these basic precautions.

- Keep your design to a small surface footprint. Designs with smaller footprints are more difficult to find whether the threat is on foot or in the air.
- Keep your structures to low profiles whenever possible. Tall objects cast large shadows, which cause them to stand out. A fully buried bunker is more advisable.
- Stay away from metal roofs. Earth or asphalt shingles don't reflect radar.
- Find a location under a natural canopy, if possible. Tree canopies can make it nearly impossible to be detected by aircraft. If the canopy is deciduous, finish your work before the leaves fall. What a disappointment it would be to work all summer long in stealth only to be detected once the leaves fall off the trees.
- Do *not* drive your 4x4 truck, golf cart, motorcycle, or any other vehicle to the bunker site or anywhere reasonably near the site. If you can drive a vehicle to your site, so can the threat. Further, vehicle tracks are perhaps the easiest tracks to spot under all circumstances. The well-hidden bunker will

not have tire tracks ending 6 feet away from the entrance. Utilize the natural paths or game trails when carrying materials and supplies in to your bunker. If there are no natural trails, carefully place natural stepping stones to walk on as you carry in your tools and materials.

- Use the native plants to conceal the bunker's roof and exposed walls. Move sod, transplant bushes, and save the topsoil from the excavation site to be replaced and blended with the undisturbed areas around your bunker.
- Position the entrance away from a likely direction of approach and conceal it from a direct line of sight. Choose locations behind hills or in slight depressions or valleys.
- Keep the actual finished walkway narrow and allow the natural grasses or brush to grow up around the path. A natural tunnel at the ground under some brambles or rose bushes would also be easily overlooked by a passerby.
- If the bunker is in the open, be certain not to kill the grass at the entrance by continually walking on the same path.

Keeping your bunker project small has many advantages, low cost being just one of them.

This shelter is just a few steps away from being well hidden from view.

This WWII German hidden position was no doubt an outpost in an open field. Note the pile of grass to the left used to further conceal the roof and the framed opening. When covered, this position would have been difficult to observe both from the air and perhaps even from across the field.

When properly hidden and kept secret, a bunker such as this may never be detected. One room, earth-covered log cabins set into a remote hillside can be very comfortable places to live with enough blankets and sweaters.

THE STORM SHELTER BUNKER

Wherever there are tornadoes, you'll find the corner bargain storm shelter set up for your inspection. Most are very simple structures with lockable door, air vent, and room to seat the average family in modest comfort. They might even have an optional LED lighting system and a weather radio available. Your expected stay in one of these might be for just a few minutes as the tornado plows through your living room or even for up to a day or so while a severe storm system spawning multiple tornadoes moves slowly through your area. Under most circumstances, having a home storm shelter is a good thing. They are truly lifesaving structures, and anyone who can afford one should have one to protect their family.

Many survivalists believe a storm shelter would make a good bunker. These structures are generally small in their footprint, watertight, include an outside air vent, and have a door that can be hidden easily. When doing research for this book, however, I researched several storm shelter systems to gain a general idea of the big picture and was surprised at what I learned.

Few companies will sell a storm shelter unit to an individual to install himself. There are several stated reasons for this. There are the typical concerns, such as the proper installation and ventilation of the shelter that are indeed warranted concerns; however, anyone who can follow directions should still be able to install his own storm shelter. It is the not-often-stated concern that prevents private individuals from installing their own premanufactured shelters. The bottom line is that FEMA demands to know the exact location and specs of your storm shelter and have a minimum of 14 photographs taken at critical points of construction as photographic evidence that the unit was not altered from the original design, used in another manner, or intended for another purpose. Further, the photographs, along with GPS coordinates, are kept to identify the exact location of the shelter. For some, this may be a good thing. After all, wouldn't you want FEMA to arrive just in time to save you from your shelter?

These storm shelters are tough and durable and could save
your life if violent weather hits. But FEMA regulations
make them a poor choice for those who desire secrecy.

This may not be what the smiling salesman will tell you, unless you continue to press that you will be doing the installation yourself. You will more likely be told that they need to do the installation, and you can have copies of the great photos they'll be taking because they like to document their work, and you may never know about the FEMA paperwork. After all, who really knows if you can be trusted?

While most storm shelters may be too small for full-time use, they can be large enough for storage and short stays for a small family or group. They could also be a type of escape pod if well concealed and properly supplied. Another use might be to use them as the front room of a larger bunker.

THE PRACTICAL USE OF SURROUNDING RESOURCES

Bunkers and protective shelters have always been a part of warfare. From the earliest times, fighters have either sought out hardened locations, such as caves or natural rock formations, to use for protection, or they have built the necessary structures with the surrounding materials available to them. Standing armies have generally had the funds and resources to build elaborate concrete and steel bunkers for their officers and left the rank and file soldiers to build field fortifications out of whatever materials they could find. Partisans make do with whatever they can find as well.

Don't overlook the common city storm drain as an emergency refuge.

Since most of today's preppers and survivalists do not have unlimited resources and military training, I'd expect most of them would follow the soldier's or partisan's methods of building bunkers.

American towns and cities are rich with opportunities to improvise bunkers, shelters, and fighting positions. Commonly found concrete storm drains and culverts can readily offer immediate protection and, with slight modifications, can be transformed into a dry-weather shelter or fighting position. Of course, depending upon the severity of your situation, storm drains can be used in wet weather as well. In fact, many cities have an underground community of sorts, where sometimes hundreds of homeless people live full-time in the protection of the storm drains.

WWII saw the construction of bunkers in nearly every type of environment around the world. Bunkers were built in open fields and deserts, sandy beaches and jungles, as well as dense forests and in towns. The photos in this section show actual examples of WWII bunkers and shelters.

A below-grade bunker entranceway has sidewalls that are held in place by a concrete or mortar patch. There is a woven ladder or ramp at the entrance end.

This WWII German bunker is nothing more than a small log cabin with an earthen roof. Smoke coming from the chimney at the wrong time might have given away the position.

Located in what appears to be in the middle of town, perhaps at the edge of a park and clearly the town's rally point, this bunker/pillbox stands ready.

Unlike their German counterparts shown in the previous photos, the Japanese weren't much for taking souvenir photos while standing outside their bunkers. The Japanese bunkers here were all located on sandy beaches and islands. They were concrete and steel in construction and buried with sand. Grasses were easily placed in the sand and helped to conceal the bunkers from air reconnaissance. Tall structures that could cast shadows easily seen from the air were avoided.

THE HOME-BUILT BURIED BUNKER

Anyone who has built a house or framed a shed can build a small wood-framed bunker. The biggest issue will be digging the hole. First, decide how wide your bunker will be, keeping in mind that the wider the bunker, the larger the roof/earth supports will have to be and the greater the cost.

The hole can be dug into a hillside with one wall toward daylight, or as a pit, like a swimming pool. Either way you'll need to follow these general guidelines to avoid having water issues.

Dealing with drainage *before* your bunker floods is always the best policy. No matter what size your underground bunker is, water can make your stay there miserable.

The worst place you can choose for your underground bunker's location is alongside a river or lake where the water table is close to the surface. A spot in which rock outcrops are visible above the surface or found near the surface would be another poor choice for several reasons.

Hopefully, your well-chosen lot has several elevated, dry areas away from the natural barrier of the river. A lot that drains well enough to support a septic system would generally be a

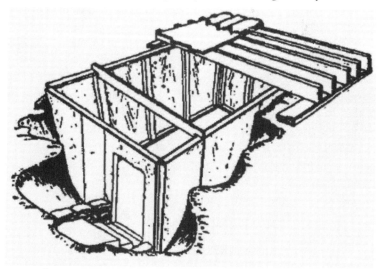

This cutaway illustration shows a bunker built into a hillside.

good lot for an underground bunker; however, there are alternate methods of construction that can protect you on any lot.

If you are uncertain about the soil and drainage qualities of your land, take the time to investigate for signs. After a rain, check the lot for areas that dry faster than others. An area that does not dry as fast as nearby areas may indicate subsurface rocks or an underground spring. Move to the dry areas. Dig a hole at your chosen site and do an inspection of the soil. Sandy soil drains well, but hard or clay-like soil can present problems. A quick percolation, or perc, test could also be done. You don't need to get too scientific here since you are not applying for a permit; you're just concerned about how fast water will drain from the area you plan to use.

Dig your perc-test hole to about a foot less than the depth of the soil you'll need to cover your bunker. That is, if the roof on the bunker is to be 3 feet underground, dig your test hole to a depth of 2 feet. Fill the hole with water and watch to see how long it takes for the hole to drain. If it is slow to drain or does not drain at all, you may need to use alternative measures or find a new location altogether.

Alternatives include building the bunker at a higher elevation or at the surface and then covering it with a man-made hill of earth and plants.

Another alternative would be to place a roof of plastic sheathing over the entire area to divert surface water away from your underground bunker. The sheathing would have to be buried and concealed as well, and would greatly increase the size of the project.

Other alternative methods include taking extra care in placing a drain field below the bunker to ensure positive drainage of any water that finds its way to your underground lair. Positive drainage can be obtained by either installing sump pumps (which can be purchased in a 12V DC model) or by running a level to down-sloping perforated drain line to the nearest break in the hill to daylight.

When excavating for the bunker, follow these basic rules:

- Do not disturb any more earth than is necessary to build your structure; avoid excavating the hole any more than 1–2 feet larger than the actual size of your structure. For instance, if the footprint of your bunker is 6x12 feet, the cut into the hillside should not be any larger than 8x14 feet.
- Clear the sidewalls of loose debris, dirt clogs, and roots that might rub the sides of the bunker.
- Before building the floor of the structure, place a layer of clean (washed), crushed stone, around 5/8-inch in size, from your local quarry as a base.
- Take the time now to lay any drainpipes or electrical conduit you intend on using. This is the time to place a perforated drainpipe around the perimeter of your bunker's base and run it to daylight. Also, a sink with a drain can be a welcome addition to your bunker even if the water comes from a jug.
- The base of stone should be about 8–10 inches deep, leveled and compacted. It should be spread wall-to-wall in the excavation cut.
- Use 90-pound rolled roofing with roofing tar at the seams for the exterior siding of your walls.
- Once the structure is built in the opening of the hillside, backfill the gaps left between the exterior walls and the excavation cut with more of your clean (washed), crushed stone backfill.
- Before burying the open side of the excavation cut, continue digging two deeper trenches, cut gently sloping downhill and toward the daylight side. Lay perforated drainage pipe from the end of the trenches, connecting to the drainage pipe under the floor.
- Keep the drainpipe running downhill from the bunker and dig a drainage pit the size of a 55-gallon drum where the drainpipe ends. The pit should be filled with stone, covered with dirt, and concealed with grass or native plants.

Once the excavation is done, the perforated pipe has been laid, and the stone has been leveled and tamped, you are ready to start framing the floor.

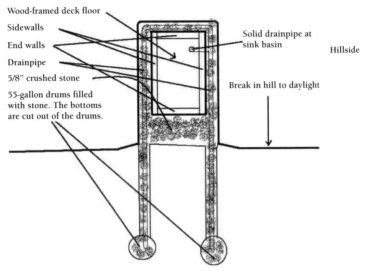

Wood-framed deck floor

Sidewalls

End walls

Drainpipe

5/8" crushed stone

55-gallon drums filled
with stone. The bottoms
are cut out of the drums.

Solid drainpipe at
sink basin

Hillside

Break in hill to daylight

Overhead view of bunker.

Working in a cramped hole can be difficult when swinging a hammer. Whenever conditions allow, consider framing in the open alongside the excavation and moving the framed components into the excavation a piece at a time.

The floor deck will be the most difficult to do this with, but with a small enough plan, it can be done.

- Once the floor deck is framed and covered with your plywood flooring, placed in the hole, and leveled on the bed of crushed stone, you can frame the bunker sidewalls.
- Again, do your framing outside of the hole on a flat surface. Nail the sheathing/plywood siding to the framed walls with an overhang at the sill that will cap the outside of the deck.
- The sidewalls should run end-to-end of the floor deck, and your end-walls should fit inside the opening left by the sidewalls.
- Longer bunkers should have an inner bulkhead wall for added lateral support.

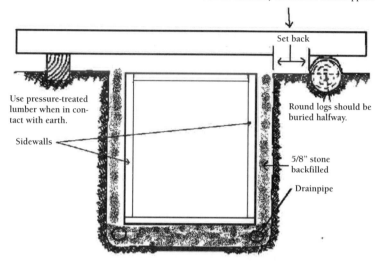

A cutaway side view of a wooden bunker.

Any of the styles or designs of the wooden bunkers shown in this section can be used above or below ground. The weight of the earth above the bunker is carried by the railroad ties, timbers, or logs spanning from side to side, well past the excavation-cut opening.

THE SHIPPING CONTAINER BUNKER

A favorite discussion in the prepper/survivalist community has been about the use of shipping containers as bunkers. It is a fact that the military has already done this with their standard containers, which are a smaller version of the 20- or 40-foot containers available to civilians.

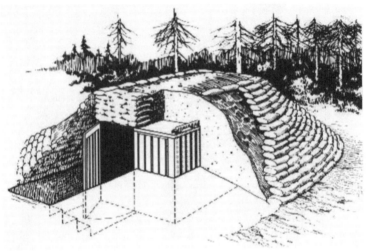

This sturdy shelter is made from a buried shipping container.

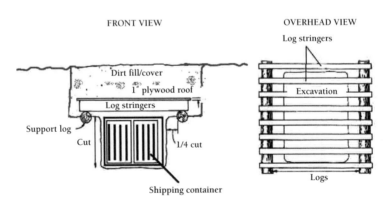

This shipping container is buried deep enough
so that the ground remains level above it.

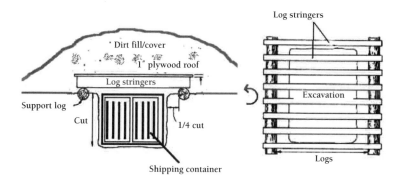

The top of this shipping container is level with the ground, requiring a berm of earth over the bunker.

Always being in a hurry, the military didn't want to take the time to reinforce the roof of the container to carry the extra weight of the dirt and sandbags. But recognizing that the floor of the container was over-engineered and made of heavy timber, they flipped the container upside down and buried it.

Depending on your situation, the 20- or 40-foot shipping container can be used as an underground shelter. It can also be used without flipping it upside down as the military does.

Both the 20- and 40-foot containers are 8 feet in width. Using the table "Center-to-Center Spacing for Wood Stringers/Beams Supporting Earth Cover to Defeat Contact Burst" on page 90, you'll be able to determine what size beams at what spacing to carry the overhead load you plan to have. The cut will have to be similar to one of the illustrations of buried shipping containers shown in this section. Building structural bulkheads or walls at several locations inside the container will also add to the stoutness of the sidewalls and roof. Consider using as many as two bulkheads in the 20-foot container and five in the 40-footer. They can be framed and welded in steel or wood and installed after the container is placed in the hole, but before the backfill is done.

THE CONCRETE BUNKER

The concrete bunker, as shown in the photos from the U.S. Army Heritage and Education Center in this section, offers a simple, hardened fighting position. The entrance is located approximately 75 yards away from the emplacement with a corrugated metal culvert pipe and a doglegged tunnel running in between. The concrete work was done at the entrance, to fortify the doorway from unwanted visitors, and at the bunker itself. The tunnel is a simple trench cut in the ground with a wood-framed walkway, capped with a split metal culvert pipe. Once the pipe is placed to cap the wooden walkway, the soil from the excavation is used to cover and bury the tunnel.

All three elements of this bunker require special attention in construction.

The bunker entrance should be set up as a hidden, defensive fighting position itself, offering some type of protective cover for those going in and out. It's no good to step out of the door and be cut down by gunfire. The door should also have a peephole installed. The entrance should face or open toward your primary direction of retreat or escape.

Tunnels can be large enough to walk in or so small that the prepper must crawl to gain access to the bunker. Some bunkers have tunnels that run deep and lead to a heavily concealed area, while others just have a back door. Let your plan for safe cover from gunfire be your guide. Ideally, the tunnel should not be a straight run, but rather angled at one or more points to help avoid detection.

The best tunnels are the ones so well concealed that the threat cannot look at the bunker and determine where the entrance is. For this reason, a deep crawl tunnel might prove to be the best since it can be the easiest to conceal. Whole-pipe tunnels that run from separate structures at your retreat are also easy to conceal.

Corrugated plastic pipes can also be used as bunker tunnels.

This concrete pillbox bunker affords a highly
effective fighting position. A corrugated metal pipe creates a
75-yard tunnel between the bunker and the entrance.

THE DUMMY BUNKER

Trickery and deception can be powerful tools in battle, where decisions are often made based only on visual intelligence gathered from the field. Cutout figures have been used successfully to deceive the threat since World War II. How many times have you slowed down in your car because you caught a glimpse of a deer or a bear, only to later learn it was just a life-sized, black-painted silhouette in a neighbor's yard? Several life-sized silhouettes of men at the windows or inside a doorway throughout your house can give the illusion of a 24-hour watch. A group of tents inside a compound may actually be empty, but to a distant outside observer it could suggest the presence of a large group. Similar ruses can also be used around the retreat.

A plywood perimeter bunker.

A fake, or dummy, bunker can be used nearly anywhere. Consider where you'd like to see the attackers concentrate their resources and attention and place a fake bunker there. You might place one adjacent to a well-concealed fighting position to take some of the fire off your position.

For those preppers who expect a more sophisticated threat that would employ the use of thermal imaging technologies, a

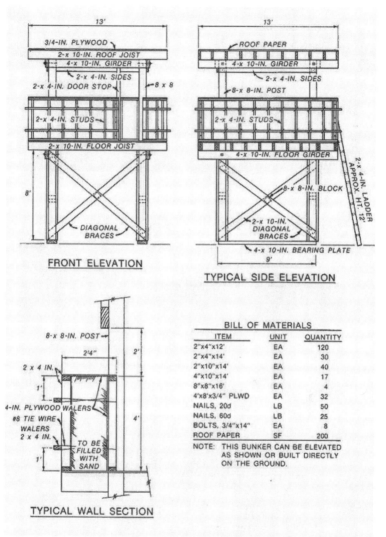

Building plan for a plywood perimeter bunker.

BILL OF MATERIALS			
NO.	ITEM	UNIT	QUANTITY
1	CAP OR SILL 6x8x8'-0"	EA	4
2	POST 6x6x 5'-10"	EA	6
3	STRINGER* 6x6x6'-0"	EA	16
4	SPREADER 3x6x5'-0"	EA	5
5	POST, DOOR 3x6x6'-3"	EA	1
6	BRACE**3x6x 7'-0"	EA	1
7	BRACE**3x6x 6'-10"	EA	2
8	BRACE***3x6x 8'-0"	EA	2
9	SPREADER 2x6x3'-3"	EA	6
10	SPREADER 2x6x2'-9"	EA	2
11	SPREADER 2x6x2'-0"	EA	2
12	SLAB 2x6x 1'-0"	EA	2
13	SIDING 3xRWx8'-0"	SQ FT	92
14	SIDING 3xRWx6'-0"	SQ FT	39
15	SIDING 3xRWx3'-6"	SQ FT	23
16	ROLL ROOF- ING (100 SQ FT ROLL)	SQ FT	600
17	DRIFTPIN (1/2"x14")	EA	44
18	NAILS (60d)	LB	32

* LAMINATED WOOD ROOF MAY BE SUB- STITUTED IF DESIRED. WHEN CON- NECTING TWO MODULES STRINGERS MAY BE 6 x 6 x 12'-0" (16 REQ'D).

** ALLOWANCE FOR DOUBLE OUT ENDS OF BRACES IS INCLUDED IN OVERALL LENGTH AS SHOWN.

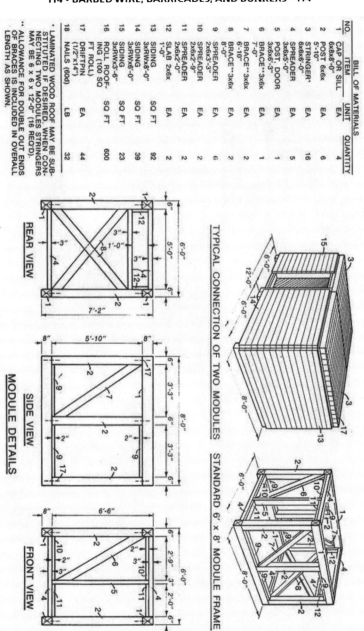

Modular timber frame shelter.

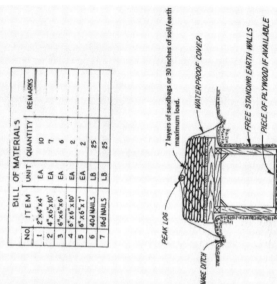

BILL OF MATERIALS

NO.	ITEM	UNIT	QUANTITY	REMARKS
1	2"x4"x4'	EA	10	
2	4"x6"x10'	EA	7	
3	6"x6"x6'	EA	6	
4	6"x6'x10'	EA	2	
5	6"x6'x7'	EA	2	
6	40d NAILS	LB	25	
7	16d NAILS	LB	25	

7 layers of sandbags or 30 inches of soil/earth maximum load.

WATERPROOF COVER

FREE STANDING EARTH WALLS

PIECE OF PLYWOOD IF AVAILABLE

BOARDS AS SUBFLOOR

PEAK LOG

DRAINAGE DITCH

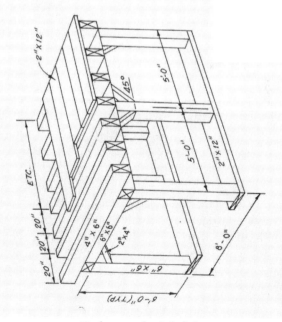

2"x12"

45°

5'-0"

5'-0"

2"x12"

ETC.

20" 20" 20"

4" X 6"

6" X 6"

2" X 4"

6" X 6"

8' - 0"

8'-0" (TYP.)

Timber-post buried shelter.

A deep box with the inside bottom painted black gives the illusion of being the rifle port of a bunker.

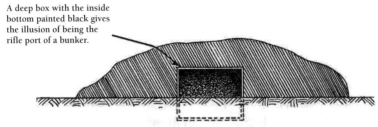

The excess dirt from excavating other structures can be used to construct dummy bunkers or fighting positions to lure the enemy away from other points of interest. Use natural grass and plants to a lesser degree than your actual positions.

wood-framed layer, filled with compost or a leaf and manure mix, should create enough of a temperature differential to confirm the bunker's existence. The 2x8 frame should be open at the top and bottom and be placed approximately 24 inches below the surface.

With enough fake bunkers, the attackers won't know what is real or fake and may slow the attack until their true exposure is determined. Or they may get reckless and push into the unknown. With proper planning, you can take advantage of either situation.

SOME PROVEN VARIATIONS

The illustrations in this section detail some field-proven plans that are simple structures that offer protection. Like the plywood perimeter bunker, they are just variations on a few simple designs. The differences are more about what materials are available or what your specific needs are than which is a better structure. The elevated bunker may appear to be worthless in an open, flat-land area but, makes more sense when placed behind a hill where the line of sight allows full observation over the hill and the hill itself offers protection to the base of the structure.

Determine which structures will benefit you the most by weighing the expected threats and your location's natural features.

Chapter Eleven

Thoughts and Conclusions

•

Choice is the essence of freedom. Those who wait too long to make their choices may lose that freedom — and have those choices made for them by others.

The measures and structures discussed in this book can be expensive to implement for many preppers. Money will continue to be short for all, and inflationary pressures will no doubt continue as well.

But by using what is readily available, most preppers should, at the very least, be able to find a remote or hidden location that can be used as a rally point for immediate family members to wait safely for the arrival of the others. Caches can be placed at such locations and successful escapes from larger threats can be made. Some preppers may even be able to construct a hidden bunker for continued use, while still more will consider fortifying their home retreats and making plans to stand in place against threats that are expected to arrive.

The most important conclusion that can be drawn from the information reviewed is that keeping as much ground between you and the expected threat is the best policy. This can be interpreted to mean ground as in distance or ground as in dirt or earth.

The use of barbed wire and bollards in keeping threats away from your location is second only to having a well-stocked, hidden bunker with three or more feet of earth offering protection from radiation, small arms fire, flamethrowers, and direct bursts of 120mm guns.

It is my hope that this short essay illustrates and conveys the concepts and ideas necessary to fortify the home retreat against coming threats, whatever they may be. Your personal survival may rest with the information in this book.

About
the
Author

•

F.J. Bohan has been a survivalist since his late teens and continues to be one today.

After 30 years of experience, he believes that the two key ingredients for survival are clean water and the information that can be found in books. Whether talking about the survival chances of an individual or mankind as a whole, the technical threats that exist today demonstrate that the survivalist must own an extensive library of books and have them in hard-copy form to prevent that information from being lost to an EMP, solar flare, Internet shut-down, or an oppressive government.

F.J. lives with his wife in the American Appalachians, where the water flows freely.